KONSEP BOOKS
KONSEP LAGENDA SDN BHD (223 855)
Kuala Lumpur 59100, MALAYSIA

Email: fengshui@lillian-too.com.
WEBSITE: www.lillian-too.com

LILLIAN TOO'S PERSONALIZED FENG SHUI TIPS
© Konsep Lagenda Sdn Bhd

ISBN 983 9778 – 07 - 2

First published June 1998
Reprinted seven times
This reprint January 1999
9th reprint April 1999

Printed by Ritz Print S/B
Kuala Lumpur
Malaysia

LILLIAN TOO'S PERSONALIZED FENG SHUI TIPS

Personalized TIPS to ...
* make your house auspicious
* enhance your personal space
* maximize your career luck
* magnify your success potential

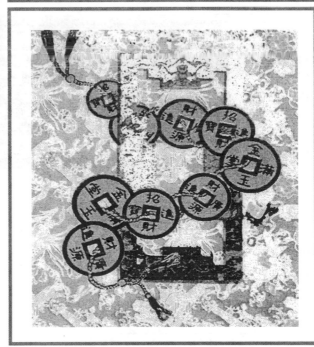

With utmost reverence and respect for
**The most Venerable
Lama Zopa Rinpoche**

And for
JENNIFER

Visit the world's first completely online
FENG SHUI MAGAZINE at
www.worldoffengshui.com

Meet Lillian Too

In retirement she has become the world's number ONE selling writer on a subject that is taking the world by storm - FENG SHUI. Her books on Feng shui have penetrated every corner of the globe. She has made bestseller lists in USA, UK, Germany, Holland, Norway, South Africa, Australia and of course Malaysia and Singapore. In the UK, USA and in Singapore her books have reached **number ONE** in the Bestseller charts. Currently her latest offering **LILLIAN TOO's LITTLE BOOK OF FENG SHUI** has been number ONE in the UK Bestseller charts for over eight weeks.

Her feng shui books have been **translated into fifteen languages** – German, French, Spanish, Greek, Italian, Polish, Japanese, Indonesian, Slovenian, Portuguese, Swedish, Russian, Norwegian, Czechoslovakian and Hungarian. She has **sold well over a million copies of her** books worldwide and today is constantly invited to speak on feng shui in five continents. In **Malaysia** where she comes from, Lillian Too is described by **Malaysian Business**, the country's leading business magazine as
"... *Something of a legend in corporate circles being the first woman there to become the Managing Director of a publicly listed company* "
Lillian is an MBA graduate from the **Harvard Business School,** in Boston USA; She has been described as being *"in a league of her own "* by the country's leading **SUCCESS** magazine. The internationally acclaimed **VOGUE** magazine describes her " *as someone people listen to..*
Lillian Too is married and has one daughter.

Other books by Lillian Too

PUBLISHED BY
KONSEP LAGENDA SDN BHD

* Feng Shui
* Applied Pa Kua Lo Shu Feng Shui
* Practical Applications of Feng Shui
* Water Feng Shui for Wealth
• Dragon Magic - my feng shui stories
* Chinese Astrology for Romance and Relationships
• Lillian Too's Basic Feng shui
• Lillian Too's Flying Star Feng shui
* The Chinese Dragon
* Strategies for Career Success
* Creative Visualization
* Tap the Power Inside You
* Explore the Frontiers of your Mind

PUBLISHED BY ELEMENT BOOKS
U.K, Australia and USA

* The Complete Illustrated Guide to Feng Shui.
* FENG SHUI Fundamentals series of nine books:
Feng shui in eight easy lessons;
Feng shui for Love; Feng shui for Education;
Feng shui for Networking; Feng shui for Career,
Feng shui for Children; Feng shui for Health;
Feng shui for Fame; Feng shui for Wealth.
The Complete Illustrated Guide to FENG SHUI for GARDENS
Lillian Too's Little Book of Feng Shui

PUBLISHED BY RIDER BOOKS,
RANDOM HOUSE, UK

* Feng Shui Essentials

Opening notes ...

It has been five years since I wrote my first feng shui book to introduce this magnificent practice to the world, and to preserve a valuable heritage and tradition of the Chinese people. I certainly did not realize then that feng shui would soon capture the acceptance of the world, that it would cross all the great waters of the earth and find fertile soil to take root, grow and blossom in so many foreign lands. That it has become so popular in so many countries, is due to it being a practice that really does improve lives and luck at little cost and effort !

Many wonderful people are responsible for this revival of interest in feng shui ...old masters, traditional practitioners and new age enthusiasts. Many writers have played valuable roles in spreading the vogue of feng shui, by unselfishly sharing their knowledge and promoting this ancient practice – in the process, enhancing and improving the lives of many people. I salute especially the pioneer writers who, many years ago shared their fledgling discovery of feng shui with the English speaking world. Writers like Derek Walters, Stephen Skinner, Sarah Rossbach, Kwok Man Ho, Evelyn Lip and Raymond Lo to name but a few. Today there are many more engaged in disseminating what they have learnt from localized masters and old practitioners. Some of course do it better than others, and some are more genuinely authentic than others, but all play a valuable role in increasing awareness of this wonderful practice.

Basic Feng shui is easy to learn. But it is a subject that has great breadth of formulas and incredible depth of analysis and practice. For me personally, the continuos availability of greater and in-depth information that comes my way to aid me in my study of the subject continues to astound me. I am also guided in my writing by the sheer number of letters and emails I get – some few hundred a week. These communications from my readers give me feedback that really helps me improve explanations of all the feng shui recommendations I offer.

This book is in response to the growing demand for personalized feng shui tips that are easily understood and incorporated into daily living. In putting together this book, I have called on my store of old books and notes on feng shui. I have also incorporated many cultural do's and don'ts I had previously dismissed as superstition but which I now realize manifest oral transmissions of an ancient wisdom passed down to me by my own ancestors. I loved writing this book, choosing the words, drawing the pictures and designing the pages to make it good to look at, easy to read and simple to use ... I genuinely hope something inside this book brings every reader the good fortune they each want.

What others say ....

" ... Too distills the essence of the practice and explains
in simple terms how feng shui can improve anyone's life ..."
VOGUE magazine

" Too's credentials are impeccable"
SARAWAK SUNDAY TRIBUNE

" ... to the readers of her best selling books throughout Malaysia,
Lillian Too has only just begun "
BUSINESS TIMES

" ... Lillian Too is something of a legend in Malaysian corporate circles ...
with a formidable cv... " MALAYSIAN BUSINESS

" ... Too is a person who practices what she preaches "
NEW STRAITS TIMES

" ... she is not the sort of proponent of this ancient Chinese art who
peddles her knowledge to companies ... what she does, and has done
with considerable success, is write books about feng shui ... "
SMART INVESTOR

" Lillian Too's feng shui site has been big news. Feng shui is the Chinese
art of geomancy - a cross between psychic energy and interior design -
and Lillian Too can make a Swiss ski chalet seem as spiritual as
Stonehenge ... in Asia she is a celebrity and her online consultations are
burning up lots of Asian band - width ..."
WIRED, USA

" Highly readable and with interesting anecdotes, Lillian Too's FENG SHUI
should interest everyone who seeks to understand the forces of Nature ...
it is an invaluable addition to the growing literature on Eastern thinking and
Lillian Too is to be congratulated for her timely contribution ... "
Dr Tarcisius Chin, CEO
MALAYSIAN INSTITUTE OF MANAGEMENT

What others say ....

... An interesting read
I found myself looking at my flat in a totally different way"
The OBSERVER newspaper London on
Lillian Too's FENG SHUI FUNDEMENTALS

... With great illustrations and clear explanations, Lillian Too demonstrates
how to make the best of our living spaces and offers plenty of tips to
improve energy flows immediately."
PREVIEW magazine, UK gives
Lillian Too's FENG SHUI IN EIGHT EASY LESSONS a five star rating.

This is a book to guide you through FENG SHUI's roots ... its principles and
practice ... how to harness energy lines and live in harmony with your
environment.
UK'S COUNTRY LIVING
on The Complete Illustrated Guide to Feng Shui ...

... Donald Trump, Olivia Newton John and Boy George have all had their
homes feng shui-ed by experts... BUT Lillian Too's Feng shui Kit contains
all you need to do it yourself.
The Saturday MIRROR, UK
on LILLIAN TOO'S FENG SHUI KIT

"Lillian Too's FENG SHUI is outstanding and spellbinding in more ways
than one. Here is a piece of work that has been well researched and
represents what the writer has "soaked up" from books and practitioners.
The well matched marriage between theory and practice contributes to the
comprehensiveness of the book. Yet there is no false pretensions on the
part of the writer ... the reader's interest is sustained throughout the book.
I highly recommend this book for both practitioners and non practitioners ".

Professor Dr. Leong Yin Ching PhD (London)
Professor of Education UNIVERSITY OF MALAYA

CHAPTER ONE
FENG SHUI IN THE HOME

CHAPTER TWO
FENG SHUI IN ALL YOUR RELATIONSHIPS

CHAPTER THREE
FENG SHUI IN YOUR OFFICE

TIPS FOR ENHANCING YOUR WORK SPACE

TIPS FOR PERSONALIZED OFFICE ARRANGEMENTS

LUCKY AND UNLUCKY OBJECTS

CHAPTER FOUR
FENG SHUI TO BOOST YOUR CAREER

CHAPTER FIVE
FENG SHUI FOR BETTER WEALTH LUCK

CHAPTER SIX
TIPS FOR DIFFERENT ROOMS IN THE HOME

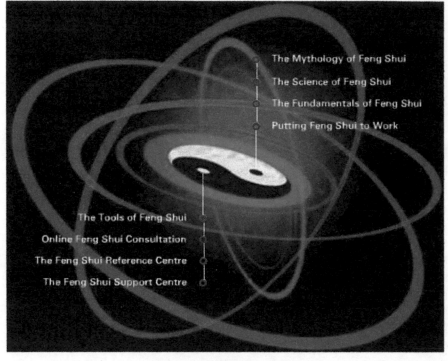

CHAPTER
ONE

FENG SHUI
IN THE
HOME

ENRICHING
YOUR
PERSONAL
SPACE

Determine your AUSPICIOUS | TIP

The best way to start in the practice of personal feng shui is to determine the four corners of your living space that are most auspicious for you. These are the luckiest spots in any room, office or apartment for you. Sitting, sleeping or working in any of these four specific locations will generally bring you good luck. And protect you from bad luck. The formula used for identifying these lucky locations is a special Compass Formula. Start by calculating your **KUA** number by following the formula here, and then refer to the table below for your most auspicious corners. Please note that these are your lucky <u>locations.</u>

The formula for determining your KUA number.
Using your *lunar** calendar year of birth, add the last two digits. Keep adding the digits until you get a single digit number. Then:
For Men, deduct this number from 10. The result is your KUA number.
For women, add this number to 5. The result is your **KUA** number.
If you get two digits keep adding until you reduce it to one digit eg. if you get the number 10 then 1+0=1; and if you get the number 14 then 1+4= 5. Refer to the Table below to find out your auspicious locations.
*this means if you were born before the lunar New Year each year you must deduct 1 from your year of birth (you need the **date** of birth to determine this since generally, this affects those born before February but it is useful to check a Lunar calendar to be exact.*

TABLE OF AUSPICIOUS CORNERS & LOCATIONS

YOUR KUA NUMBER	YOUR AUSPICIOUS CORNERS & LOCATIONS IN DESCENDING ORDER OF LUCK	INDICATING THAT YOU ARE *EAST* OR *WEST* GROUP PERSON
1	Southeast, East South, North,	East
2	Northeast. West. Northwest, Southwest	West
3	South, North, Southeast, East	East
4	North, South, East, Southeast	East
5	MEN: N.East, West, Northwest, SWest WOMEN: SWest, Northwest, West, NEast	West
6	West, Northeast, Southwest, Northwest	West
7	Northwest, Southwest, Northeast, West	West
8	Southwest, Northwest, West, Northeast	West
9	East, Southeast, North, South	East

Note: West Group CORNERS are inauspicious for East group people & vice versa

CHAPTER
ONE

FENG SHUI
IN THE
HOME

ENRICHING
YOUR
PERSONAL
SPACE

Find out your Good Fortune DIRECTIONS | TIP 2

Compass Feng shui is based on personal birth dates, and the compass points that indicate auspicious locations also indicate the best directions. Thus when orientating your sitting and sleeping directions, you must also know what your personal best directions are. Refer to the table below and memorize the directions that are auspicious for you. Then try as far as possible to always sit directly facing your most auspicious direction. In instances where this is physically not possible, you should then try to use at least one of your other three good directions. They may not be your best directions but it is infinitely better to sit facing an acceptable direction than to sit facing a direction that is inauspicious and spells total loss for you ! The Formula describes the specific types of good and bad luck of all the eight directions of the compass. These are based on individual KUA numbers and are reproduced in the Table below for easy reference.

TABLE OF AUSPICIOUS & INAUSPICIOUS DIRECTIONS

Your KUA number	1	2	3	4	5 *	6	7	8	9
AUSPICIOUS DIRECTIONS									
Your **sheng chi** I.e. your success direction	SE	NE	S	N	NE SW	W	NW	SW	E
Your **tien yi** i.e. health direction	E	W	N	S	W NW	NE	SW	NW	SE
Your **nien yen** i.e. romance direction	S	NW	SE	E	NW W	SW	NE	W	N
Your **fu wei** i.e. personal development direction	N	SW	E	SE	SW NE	NW	W	NE	S
INAUSPICIOUS DIRECTIONS									
Your **ho hai** or unlucky direction	W	E	SW	NW	E S	SE	N	S	NE
Your **wu kwei** or five ghosts direction	NE	SE	NW	SW	SE N	E	S	N	W
Your **lui sha** Or six killings direction	NW	S	NE	W	S E	N	SE	E	SW
Your **chueh ming** Or total loss direction	SW	N	W	NE	N SE	S	E	SE	NW

* KUA number 5, the top numbers are for men, and those below are for women

2

CHAPTER
ONE

FENG SHUI
IN THE
HOME

ENRICHING
YOUR
PERSONAL
SPACE

Be aware of the energies in your SPACE | TIP 3

How can you tell if you are suffering from bad feng shui ? I have often been asked this question, and my advice has been for people to get into the habit of developing awareness to their surroundings, Be sensitive to the occurrence of things going wrong, especially when there seems to be a pattern and a frequency that seems to suggest a spate of bad luck. Shakespeare said, "*troubles come not in ones' and twos but in battalions*". He could have been describing the effect of bad feng shui. This is because bad luck that is caused by bad feng shui happens almost continuously.

The effect of unbalanced energies, or of being hit by killing breath often cause things to go wrong with no respite. Your environment and the physical structures that occupy your personal space, emanate many different kinds of energies all the time. These energies can be gross or subtle, and they are either benevolent or treacherous. In other words they can bring good luck or misfortune. So you should try to tune into the energies that surround your personal space. This does not imply becoming obsessed with feng shui. What it does mean is that you will benefit enormously if you develop sensitivity to how these energies affect your living space. The best times to "check" the feng shui of your personal space are:
1.   when you have just moved into a new home or office, and
2.   during change of years and decades e.g. during the lunar new year.

Develop awareness to the flow of energy
Consciously monitor subtle changes in the space and time dimensions of your home. Feng shui is all about changing the energies of space and time. So, observe the flow as you walk through your space. If *your flow* is meandering and leisurely, the energies will be more auspicious than if the flow is straight and fast. Too many nooks and corners will cause obstacles to your flow, and are thus bad news. Your life will not be smooth. Obstacles frequently prevent you from attaining your goals.

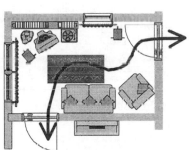

The flow is meandering.
The feng shui is good

When your flow keeps coming to a stop, the same effect occurs ... so be sensitive to how you are being made to move within your space by the way you have placed your furniture, or by the way the layout of your rooms have been designed.

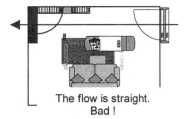

The flow is straight.
Bad !

3

CHAPTER
ONE

FENG SHUI
IN THE
HOME

ENRICHING
YOUR
PERSONAL
SPACE

Identify inauspicious structures around you | TIP 4

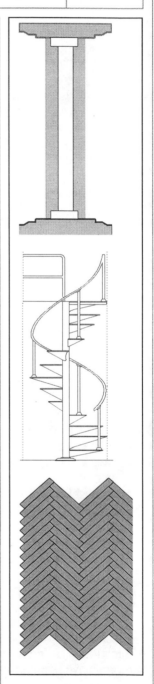

I once followed the progress of a huge mansion being built in my neighborhood. The house was enormous, and the people building it were obviously wealthy. Surely they must have consulted a feng shui master I thought, since the main front door had been oriented awkwardly, probably to tap the best direction for the residents. Sadly, the house was destined for bad luck because the front door opened directly to a decorative column (sketched here on the right). This pillar stood smack in the middle of the foyer facing the grand entrance into the home. Barely three months after they occupied the completed home, the patriarch had a heart attack, and the family business collapsed.

So always take note of every structure that occupies your space, and try to nullify their bad feng shui effects by either blocking them off from view with plants or screens or nullifying their effects with lights.

Pillars:

Structural square pillars that block doors are always bad. Wrap them with mirrors or better still, use a creeper plant to block off the sharp edges. Round pillars are not as harmful but when they directly confront your main door, they can be quite deadly. Place a screen between it and the main door.

Spiral staircases

These are really quite inauspicious structures to have around and if placed in the center of the home, they can spell disaster. The spaces in between the steps cause "money" to drain away, and the circular corkscrew effect of the shape symbolizes great damage being done to the home.

Screens

Decorative room dividers should never stand like the sketch here. They create deadly poison arrows this way. Place them straight either hanging suspended from the ceiling or firmly anchored to the ground. Screens make excellent feng shui cures especially to slow down inauspicious fast moving energy.

CHAPTER
ONE

FENG SHUI
IN THE
HOME

ENRICHING
YOUR
PERSONAL
SPACE

Counter "arrows" that hit your main door   TIP 5

No house with a main door that is hit by the killing energy of secret poison arrows can enjoy good feng shui. No matter how "correct" the directions and orientations, the color scheme and all other things, a single deadly poison arrow – anything that is pointed, sharp, straight and hostile – can destroy carefully crafted feng shui features and orientations. Thus it is vital for the feng shui practitioner to identify anything in the immediate environment, inside and outside the home, which can symbolize this poison arrow.

Exterior Poison arrows are usually more deadly and more difficult to cope with. Usually there is little one can do about the sharp edges of a neighboring building, or the triangular roof line of a neighbor's house or an oncoming straight road that seems to be aimed directly at one's main front door. Usually the best method of coping with dangerous structures that threaten one's feng shui is to re-orientate the door. Change the door direction completely or use another door and close up the afflicted door. Hanging an eight-sided Pa Kua mirror or hanging a five rod windchime to confront the structure can help to some extent, but the most effective method is to change the placement and location of the main door.

The eight sided **PA KUA** symbol shown hung above the front door is a very powerful feng shui antidote. This PA KUA is known as the yin Pa Ku, and it's power comes from its shape as well as the specially arranged sequence of trigrams placed on each of the eight sides. This special YIN arrangement is often referred to as the Early Heaven Arrangement. The mirror in the center can be convex or concave. Both versions work. Always hang the PA KUA outside the home. Never hang it inside the home, or inside the office. It has the power to destroy ALL your good feng shui inside the house. It will cause havoc inside the house. So the PA KUA mirror is used outside only and always facing away from the house !

CHAPTER
ONE

FENG SHUI
IN THE
HOME

ENRICHING
YOUR
PERSONAL
SPACE

Sleep with your head pointed correctly | TIP 6

If you have a choice of bedrooms, select the one that is located in your most auspicious <u>location</u>. This means it should be the bedroom that is located in the corner of the building that corresponds to your best direction, i.e. your *sheng chi* direction.

If it is not possible for you to have a *"sheng chi"* bedroom, try to at least get a bedroom which is located in that part of the building that corresponds to one of your four good directions. If this too is not possible, there is no need to fret since it is never possible for anyone to get everything perfect.

What you must have however is a bed that is positioned in such a way that your head is pointed towards your best direction so that while you sleep. Excellent auspicious energy is flowing into you FROM your sheng chi direction. This is a powerful method of enjoying really excellent feng shui. If you really cannot tap your sheng chi sleeping direction, again try to tap one of your four best directions. In making the decision on your bed direction, make very sure that when you arrange your bed, it does

1. not cause you to be sleeping directly under a beam
2. are not being hit by the edge of a protruding corner
3. do not have your feet directly pointed to the door
4. do not have your head or toes pointed to a toilet
5. do not have the bed headboard directly under a window.

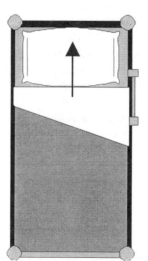

If you have a choice, always select what I call your *sheng chi* bedroom if you want success in your career or business. A *sheng chi* bedroom is one that is located in your personal *sheng chi* direction. If this is North then go for the bedroom that is placed in the north corner of your house.

At least choose a bedroom that is located in ONE of your four good directions. If this is not possible then you should try very hard to sleep with your head pointed to the North or one of the other three of your auspicious directions. It is easier to control your sleeping direction since this depends on the simple act of moving your bed until the head is pointed to the direction you want.

Refer to the tables on pages 1 and 2 to implement the tip on this page

CHAPTER
ONE

FENG SHUI
IN THE
HOME

ENRICHING
YOUR
PERSONAL
SPACE

Sit in your best feng shui position | TIP 7

Where we sit, and the direction we face while sitting create good or bad feng shui depending on what our personal KUA numbers are. Thus where we sit at work, and what direction we face while negotiating, giving a presentation, or making a speech affects our luck, often to such a significant extent it makes a difference. In the same way, how our chairs are oriented when we eat, gamble or simply socialize, can all have consequential feng shui implications.

Thus it is possible to consciously improve our luck merely by focusing on our sitting arrangement – the placement and orientation of our own chairs and tables. Thus make certain your office table and chair is positioned to capture your most auspicious directions and placement. And when you eat at home do the same thing.

In personalized feng shui I always recommend everyone I meet, to memorize their individual auspicious directions and carry a compass around so that there is never a time when one does not sit facing at least one of the four good directions.

Here are some valuable tips on how to magnify the uses of the sitting direction:

- when out on an important dinner date, and the occasion is romantic, sit facing your *nien yen* direction. It will enhance good feelings.
- When taking an exam sit facing your *fu wei* direction – it will give you the edge.
- When out at an interview or important meeting sit facing your *sheng chi* direction.It will increase your chances of success.

Note the different directions the two men are facing. Usually irrespective of which direction your chair is pointed to, it is possible to 'swivel your body to capture at least ONE of your four good directions.

Thus when you are interviewing or taking an exam or at a meeting that is not held in YOUR place, use this method to ensure that you are at least facing one of your good directions.

To implement this tip effectively you will need to memorize your auspicious directions and always carry a small compass with you wherever you go. Incorporate this tip into your practice.

Refer to the tables on pages 1 and 2 to implement the tip on this page

CHAPTER
ONE

FENG SHUI
IN THE
HOME

ENRICHING
YOUR
PERSONAL
SPACE

Good eating feng shui brings good fortune | TIP 8

One of the most wonderful features to have in your home is to install a large mirror, perhaps a wall mirror, in your dining room. This brings the best kind of eating feng shui. It symbolically doubles the food on the table. Please note however that placing a mirror next to your stove is simply NOT the same thing. When you place a mirror next to your stove you will be creating very dangerous feng shui. It leads to severe physical danger, and you could well break a leg or an arm if you do this. Mirrors in the dining room enhance your fortunes. Mirrors in the kitchen bring grave danger into your life.

Another wonderful tip to magnify eating feng shui is to hang a picture of delicious looking and ripe fruit in the dining room. Placing a bowl of fruits on the Dining table is also excellent. This recommendation creates beautiful energy that symbolizes the availability of food in the home. In the same way always make certain your refrigerator is well stocked and that you never run out of rice in your rice urn. In short never run out of basic foodstuff in your home.

A tip for lovers

If you sit facing your *nien yen* direction, the feng shui for romance, for getting a commitment from your "date" vastly improves. This is because the sitting direction energizes your family and romance luck. The nein yen direction is a very powerful feng shui tool, and you should use it only when you are very certain that you really want to activate your romance luck. You should not use it with everyone since the problems created could be bigger than you realize.

In feng shui when we speak of romance we do not mean having a fling !

When we speak of romance we mean marriage, family and commitment. You should never activate your *nien yen* direction frivolously.

Refer to the tables on pages 1 and 2 to implement the tip on this page

CHAPTER
ONE

FENG SHUI
IN THE
HOME

ENRICHING
YOUR
PERSONAL
SPACE

Take care of your rice bowl

TIP 9

The rice bowl symbolizes a family's livelihood, and Chinese families of the old tradition go to great lengths to observe certain "rules" with respect to the rice bowl. These rules were handed down by word of mouth from members of the older generation, often from grandmothers, and as such are often dismissed as superstition by the modern generation. In recent years however, interest in feng shui as a way of living harmoniously with the energies of one's personal space has encouraged a more accepting attitude towards traditional advice of this kind. Many of today's Western educated Chinese, in rediscovering their roots are practicing feng shui by carefully taking care of the family rice bowl.

TWO IMPORTANT TIPS ON THE RICE BOWL

Never eat from a rice bowl that is chipped. When the rim of the bowl is chipped, one will encounter serious problems caused by one's speech. It is advisable to throw such a bowl away and get a new one. When the bottom rim of the bowl is chipped, the negative bad luck is believed to worse since this affects the foundation of one's life. Eating from a broken bowl can cause one to lose one's job, get laid off in a recession or worse, it could lead to one's business collapsing.

Never ever stick two chopsticks standing vertically into the rice bowl, as shown here. This causes extremely severe bad luck since it symbolizes praying to the dead. Usually it is said to cause a death in the family because the yin energy created is said to be too strong. This is because two chopsticks resemble two joss sticks.

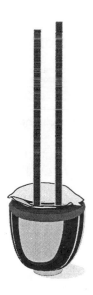

9

CHAPTER
ONE

FENG SHUI
IN
THE HOME

Personalized
Interior
Decoration

Understanding the four pillars in feng shui | TIP 10

The **FOUR PILLARS** of destiny is one of the main methods used In Chinese fortune telling The four pillars are your year, month, day and hour of birth. From this information Chinese fortune tellers calculate out what is referred to as your **EIGHT CHARACTERS**. These eight characters are the elements of feng shui – wood, water, fire, metal and fire – with a yin or a yang aspect. Each of your "pillars" corresponds to two elements which are given the names *heavenly stem* and *earthly branch*. The method of feng shui that uses the four pillars analyses each individual's eight elements and from there determine the elements that are deemed to be *"missing"* from the birth chart. Enhancing the missing elements in the personal space is believed to then strengthen the individual's feng shui.

The calculation of one's personal FOUR PILLARS and EIGHT CHARACTERS CHART is a very complicated process and does not lend itself easily to accuracy without a great deal of experience. In Hong Kong fortune tellers who use this method of calculation use a special computerized program to ensure that no mistakes are made. This is because the combinations are said to be infinite.

For feng shui purposes, my recommendation is to energize ALL the elements within the personal space. This means <u>all</u> the corners of the home and in this way ensure that all the five elements of the home are properly energized and in balance with no single element dominating. In the same way I have found that it is also an excellent idea to keep yin and yang nicely balanced for the same reason.

All the tips in this book are aimed at achieving these two fundamentals of feng shui practice.

The FIVE ELEMENTS

The five elements are WOOD, FIRE, WATER, EARTH and METAL. The elements interact in accordance to either their PRODUCTIVE or their DESTRUCTIVE cycle.

The PRODUCTIVE CYCLE

describes Wood producing Fire which produces Earth which produces Metal which produces Water which produces Wood in a never ending cycle.

The DESTRUCTIVE CYCLE

Describes Wood as destroying Earth which destroys Water which destroys Fire which destroys Metal which destroys Wood in a never ending cycle.

From the cycles you can see which elements harmonize best with another element. The creation of element rapport in the personal space is vital. You can achieve this without having to resort to the Four Pillars calculation. Using the Compass formula methods to determine your auspicious directions is sufficient.

CHAPTER
ONE

FENG SHUI
IN
THE HOME

Personalized
Interior
Decoration

Memorizing your enhancing elements | TIP 11

To personalize the feng shui of your interior décor, you can use the following table to identify the elements that are associated with different types of luck for you personally. This is based on your KUA number, which, we have seen is calculated according to your date of birth and your gender. Once you know which element is particularly auspicious for different types of luck for you, you should memorize them. Incorporate them in soft furnishings, as patterns, colors, and shapes. Use your own creativity to incorporate element feng shui.

Your KUA number	1	2	3	4	5	6	7	8	9
Your success element	Small wood	Small earth	fire	water	Small earth *Big earth	Small metal	Big metal	Big earth	Big wood
Your health element	Big wood	Small metal	water	fire	Small metal *big metal	Small earth	Big earth	Big metal	Small wood
Your romance element	Fire	Big metal	Small wood	Big wood	Big metal *small metal	Big earth	Small earth	Small metal	Water
Your education element	water	Big earth	Small wood	Big wood	Big earth * small earth	Big metal	Small metal	Small earth	fire

METAL element is also gold and silver. Circular designs reflect the metal element. Colors are metallic and white.

WATER element is usually wavy and curved, suggesting waves, droplets and clouds. Colors are blue and black.

FIRE element is usually sharp, pointed and triangular. The sun motif is fire. Colors are red, orange and bright yellows.

WOOD element is usually rectangular. Trees, plants and flowers all belong to wood element. Colors are brown and green.

EARTH element are square in shape in all the combinations. Colors of earth are beige and light yellow.

CHAPTER
ONE

FENG SHUI
IN
THE HOME

Personalized
Interior
Decoration

IDENTIFY your destructive elements

TIP 12

In the same way that you have auspicious elements that do " special" things for your luck, every individual also has elements that are deemed to be 'destructive" to their luck. Each individual has 4 bad luck elements in ascending order of seriousness and gravity. These are presented in the Table below.

The elements deemed "destructive" under this KUA formula may well contradict what you discover to be elements you need, or are deemed lucky for you under another feng shui formula. When you are confronted with a situation where advice appears contradictory, it is important to understand that elements in and of themselves alone seldom do much harm. Simply refrain from energizing the destructive elements indicated below, in that there is no need to use designs and colors that symbolize these elements for your own personal space. Thus if big wood is deemed inauspicious for you do not use green or wooden paneling in the decoration of your personal space.

Just remember that the destructive elements indicated here refer <u>ONLY</u> to your personal space, and NOT to your clothes . So even if wood is deemed inauspicious based on your KUA number and the table below, and you were born in a wood year for instance, then wearing green would still be regarded as auspicious for you. BUT having wood symbols or green in your personal space is bad. Thus note the subtleties of the place of elements in feng shui practice.

Remember also that this Table identifies your personal bad luck elements. Use them only for your own personal space – not for the whole house. Also, always factor in the destructive and productive cycles analysis. Thus any element that produces an element that is deemed unlucky for you is also bad !

Table of inauspicious elements based on your KUA numbers

Your KUA number	1	2	3	4	5	6	7	8	9
Your bad luck element	Small metal	Big wood	Big earth	Big metal	Big wood *fire	Small wood	Water	Fire	Small earth
Your five ghosts element	Small earth	Small wood	Big metal	Big earth	Small wood *water	Big wood	Fire	Water	Small metal
Your six killings element	Big metal	Fire	Small metal	Small metal	Fire *big wood	Water	Small wood	Big wood	Big earth
Your total loss element	Big earth	Water	Small earth	Small earth	Water *small wood	Fire	Big wood	Small wood	Big metal

CHAPTER
ONE

FENG SHUI
IN
THE HOME

Personalized
Interior
Decoration

Keep some goldfish ... or some carp	TIP 13

A truly great way of activating excellent feng shui luck inside the home is to keep some gold fish in an aquarium. Keep nine goldfish of which 8 should be red or golden and one should be black. If your goldfish die on you, do not fret. Simply get some more and replenish. When one's fish die we believe that they have absorbed some bad luck that was meant for a resident of the household.

Do NOT keep goldfish in the bedroom, in the toilets and in the kitchens. They are especially harmful in the bedroom and cause you to suffer material losses. Usually you could end up getting burgled or robbed. Keep your water feature either in the living room or outside the house.

From now until the year 2003, the BEST location to keep a goldfish aquarium is in the East, Southeast, North or Southwest. To identify the absolute best depends on the direction your front door faces, and the formula is too complicated to present here. Just make sure you do not keep goldfish any place else. Water features are very tricky in feng shui. Get it right and it brings enormous luck. Get it wrong and it becomes very dangerous. A third rule is to never place your water feature, and especially your carp pond on the right hand side of your main door (i.e. taking the direction from the inside facing outwards) since this causes the man of the house to have a roving eye !

CHAPTER
ONE

FENG SHUI
IN
THE HOME

Personalized
Interior
Decoration

Display auspicious calligraphy   TIP 14

The Chinese of olden days love displaying auspicious calligraphy in their homes, and especially the character "FOOK" which means "LUCK" shown here. Almost all Chinese ancestral homes throughout Asia, especially those homes that belong to wealthy Chinese families have their own versions of auspicious calligraphy. This symbolism of extreme good fortune is believed to be very potent feng shui feature. There are those who believe that this word "FOOK" should be displayed upside down to enhance the turnover of businesses.

Sometimes the auspicious calligraphy may be combined with other auspicious symbols like the fish and water motifs. Thus if water is an element that is auspicious for you, either because of your KUA number, or because you were born in a year when the heavenly stem was water or wood, then combining the word " FOOK" with water and fish would be extremely auspicious for you. This can be hung as a specially commissioned painting, or carved onto wood blocks or furniture, inlaid with mother of pearl.

THE CARP is an especially auspicious symbol to display around the home. This is because the carp symbolizes ambition as well as the potential for attaining great heights in material success and power. The carp is believed to have the ability to transform into the magnificent dragon.

Carps are thus considered very lucky.

CHAPTER
ONE

FENG SHUI
IN
THE HOME

Personalized
Interior
Decoration

Hang a painting of Peonies for love | TIP 15

The Peony is regarded as the "*king of flowers*" symbolic of great good fortune associated with women. Legend has it that the famous *Yang Kuei Fei*, reputed to be the most beautiful woman in Chinese history and concubine to the emperor decorated her bedchamber with beautiful peony flowers all through the year. Because the emperor could deny her nothing these flowers had to be specially brought to her from the South.

It is believed that if yours is a family of girls and, you as the mother, want them to marry well and find good husbands, then hanging a large picture of many peonies in the living room brings this kind of luck to the family. The living room is the best place for painting s of peonies, and the more luscious the blooms, the more magnificent will be the good fortune. Obviously if you can get hold of real peonies they would be just as auspicious if not better. In my living room, I activate the South corner with a huge pot of silk peonies, as much to decorate the hall, as to create wonderful romance luck for my daughter. If you are a single girl of marriageable age and you want to find a good husband then hang a peony just outside your bedroom door. You may also hang the painting inside your bedroom, but outside is better,

If you are already married, hanging a painting of peony inside your bedroom will make your husband more amorous. The danger here is that he could well develop a roving eye and start to develop love interests <u>outside</u> the marriage especially if the marriage is already getting boring. So be careful. I suggest if you have a peony painting, hang it in the living room – not in the bedroom. There are other less risky methods of bringing romance back into the marriage.

CHAPTER
ONE

FENG SHUI
IN
THE HOME

Personalized
interior
decoration

Create good luck with the right colors | TIP 16

Personalized interior decoration with feng shui is very much about the selection of colors, and the way these colors are combined with each other. Different colors work best for different corners of the home or room. Generally, the safest way to utilize color in feng shui is to use the following Table which gives you the dominant and secondary colors as well as the colors which should be strenuously avoided - in each of the corners of a home. Use the sketch below to help you identify the corners of your home.

SECTOR	Dominant colors	Secondary color	Taboo color
SOUTH	Red, orange	Yellow, green	Black, blue
NORTH	Black, blue	White, metallic	Yellow, beige
EAST	Green, brown	Black, blue	White, metal
WEST	White, gray	Metal, yellow	Red, orange
SOUTHEAST	Light green	Light blue	Gray, white
SOUTHWEST	Yellow, beige	Red, orange	Green, brown
NORTHEAST	Yellow, beige	Red, orange	Green, brown
NORTHWEST	White. Metal	Gray, yellow	Red, orange

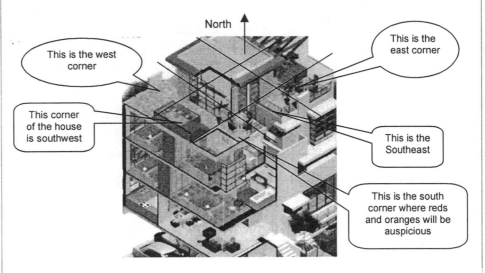

North

This is the west corner

This is the east corner

This corner of the house is southwest

This is the Southeast

This is the south corner where reds and oranges will be auspicious

The three-dimensional layout sketch of the different rooms in a multi level house shown above gives you the idea how to demarcate the different corners of a home according to the directions of a compass. Simply superimpose a nine grid rectangle over the house (as shown by the lines on the upper level in the sketch) to identify the different corners. The same direction sectors will apply to corners on every level of the house.

CHAPTER
ONE

FENG SHUI
IN
THE HOME

Personalized
Interior
Decoration

Grow an Orange or Lime Plant | TIP 17

An orange or lime plant weighed down heavily with ripening fruits symbolizes the ripening of good fortune and prosperity. Such plants are usually displayed at the entrances to doors of Chinese homes and office buildings during the fifteen days of the lunar New Year to signify a prosperous start to the New Year.

The connotation of bright red oranges also signifies gold because the sound of oranges "*kum*" also means gold. It is thus considered extreme good fortune to have plenty of oranges around during the New Year. Having a fruiting orange plant is even more auspicious.

If you grow an orange plant in your garden, plant it in the Southeast because this is the corner of your home that symbolizes wealth. Having a healthy fruiting orange plant there is extremely auspicious.

Please do not worry of the Southeast happens to be your "total loss" direction and location. When you energize or activate a corner to create the luck, which that direction symbolizes, it brings that particular good fortune to all residents. As long as you personally do not have your room in the Southeast, or sit facing the Southeast, you will also benefit.

Besides, remember that all the different methods of feng shui must complement each other. When the recommendations seem to be contradicting, think through the problem. The solution is usually not difficult to work through.

OTHER GOOD FORTUNE PLANTS
If you are a keen gardener you might wish to know that almost all plants bring good fortune to the home when they bloom and are robust. This is because of the healthy *yang* energy they create, thereby bringing prosperous activity and good business turnover. However chrysanthemums, bamboo, orchids, and plum blossoms are specifically mentioned in feng shui text books as being especially auspicious.

CHAPTER
ONE

FENG SHUI
IN
THE HOME

Personalized
Interior
Decoration

Create Curtains that bring good luck

TIP 18

1. This living room is located in the West

2. This bedroom is located in the North

ELEMENT GUIDE TO CURTAINS
South, Southwest and
Northeast: Use all shades of
red and orange. Curtains may
be angular – squares or even
triangular – but do not
inadvertently create sharp
points that hurt.
Southeast and East: Use
shades of green or brown and
make the curtains long and
rectangular looking.
West and Northwest: use
white or gray colors in the
curtains.

Curtains and all the soft furnishings of the home or office can be designed to enhance the feng shui of your personal space. One of the easiest ways of doing this is to be sensitive to the "*elements*" that should be energized in the different corners of any room, or in any of the different rooms of the home. The first thing to do is to determine what sort of room you are dealing with.

EXAMPLE 1: The top picture on the left is a West room and thus the white curtains are excellent because white, which is suggestive of the metal element is superb for the West. Next look at the shape of the curtains. They are dominantly circular and round in shape. This shape also reflects the element of metal. Here the curtains are most auspicious because they have been correctly blended in with the element of the corner it occupies. The two layers of curtains are ideal for "deflecting" excessive yang energy of the afternoon sun which shines into the West corner of any home.

EXAMPLE 2: The second picture is a bedroom that is located in the north corner of the home. The auspicious element here will be water. Thus the blue curtains are very suitable. The circular curtain pelmets suggest metal and this is excellent because metal produces water. The tiny wavy pleats of the curtain also suggest water, which complements the theme of the element of the North. Please note that energizing elements this way is different from placing physical water or hanging paintings of water in the bedroom. Use element analysis to help you create balance throughout your home. But also note the taboos along the way. Thus DO NOT place aquariums or plants in the bedroom.

CHAPTER
ONE

FENG SHUI
IN
THE HOME

Personalized
Interior
Decoration

Sleep on an authentic feng shui bed | TIP 19

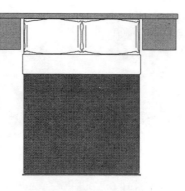

You should use the feng shui ruler to select auspicious dimensions.

An auspicious feng shui bed has *auspicious dimensions*; and is decorated in colors that harmonize with the sleeper's year element OR the element of the corner in which it is placed. Thus if you were born in a *fire* year, then shades of red would suit you, BUT not too red. Or if your bed were placed in the East corner of the bedroom, then shades of green would be very suitable. When in doubt on which system to use, I follow the element of the corner. This makes the bed generally auspicious for <u>both</u> my husband and I since we both have different year elements. But because we both sleep in the corner that has been enhanced by the correct harmonizing color we both benefit. If your bed is in the fire corner be careful that you do not make the fire element too strong. Too much yang energy in the bedroom is bad.

Beds that have a *Headboard* are much better than those without. These headboards can be made of wood, metal or padded foam. Again when deciding between a lacquered wooden bed and a brass bed, go with the element of the corner where the bed is placed. Also please note that curved and circular headboards are metal; rectangular headboards are wood or earth element, triangular headboards are fire element and wavy headboards are water element.

Bedspreads that are dark in color are to be preferred over bedspreads that are lighter in colour. Plain colored bedspreads are to be preferred to pattern designs if you are unsure of what could be harmful. Generally however I warn against selecting bedspread designs that have abstract prints or have patterns that have triangular or pointed symbols. Such fire related symbolism is usually discouraged for the bedroom, which is supposed to be a place of rest. Fire transmits yang energy, which is not so suitable for sleep. In the bedroom it would be preferable to allow yin energies to dominate, although <u>not</u> to an extent that can be harmful.

CHAPTER
ONE

FENG SHUI
IN
THE HOME

Personalized
Interior
Decoration

Let your carpets create solid foundations | TIP 20

The feng shui of your floor relate to the foundation of your life. This principle has important feng shui connotations, and in respect of personalized interior decoration there are some ground rules on carpets that can be incorporated into home decor.

Firstly, let all your carpets blend with the elements of the room where they are placed. This depends on the compass direction corner of the room where the carpet is placed in. The ruling element helps you choose the color, shape and combinations thereof, for your carpet..

Secondly, except with wall to wall carpeting let carpets reflect the general shape of the room. This creates balance and harmony. Shown above is a carpet that mirrors the energy of the room thereby allowing the room's foundations to be firmly in line with the rest of the room. This suggests that rectangular carpets are always to be preferred to round or oval carpets.

Thirdly, do not have carpets that are have busy patterns and design. These cause energies to get confused. Carpets that have exquisite and elaborate detailing (eg the stunning Persians) are not to be construed as being in this category. It is the abstract designs that can create masses of uncertainty , which in turn can cause problems.

Finally, do not place carpets on the wall. An object that is generally associated with the ground is best left on ground. This guideline becomes especially important to observe if many different people have stepped upon the exquisite carpet you have just bought, while in the shop.
If it is an antique masterpiece whose provenance and history you know nothing about you need to be even more careful. To hang such a carpet on your wall or be given a place of honor in your living room could well bring accumulated negative vibrations into your home. So be careful.

CHAPTER
ONE

FENG SHUI
IN
THE HOME

Personalized
interior
decoration

Feng shui tips on flowers in the home | TIP 21

FRESH FLOWERS
bring delightful energies into the home but also be careful ....

In the living room fresh flowers create enormously refreshing and fresh yang energy and this brings good vibes into the home. Flowers are extremely useful in creating good feng shui. But there are some basic guidelines to observe; otherwise what is good feng shui can quickly become transformed into a source of bad energy. This is because there is nothing worse than wilting or rotting flowers.

Thus, fresh flowers should be thrown out as soon as they start to fade. For the same reason I always advise against displaying or using dried flowers in flower arrangements. I would rather have fake flowers than dried flowers since the fake flowers symbolize yang and life energy while the dried flowers represent yin and dead energy. Remember that anything dead or decaying creates an excess of negative yin energy.

Flowers can be used to enhance or reduce the *yang* energies of a room. Generally speaking, flowers do not bring suitable feng shui for bedrooms, They are better suited to living rooms and dining rooms. I do not recommend the use of flowers for enhancing the feng shui of any bedroom, in the same way that I do not recommend the placement of live plants in the bedroom. This is because flowers and plants bring yang energies into the bedroom, and this often makes the bedroom excessively yang. Having said that, precisely because fresh flowers are so yang, they are extremely suitable for sick or convalescing people. In such a situation flowers are excellent for the bedroom. The giving of flowers is also considered auspicious since again it brings precious yang energy to the recipient.

CHAPTER
ONE

FENG SHUI
IN THE
HOME

Personalized
Interior
Decoration

The Feng shui of plants in the home | TIP 22

CACTUS PLANTS

Do avoid placing cactus plants inside the office or the home. No matter how tempting the beautiful cactus blooms are, they do not compensate for the bad energy created by the deadly thorns of the plant. When placed in the home or office (on windowsills and ledges) prickly cactus plants always create tiny slivers of poisonous energy that, over time cause illness, misfortunes and losses.

Cactus plants are best placed OUTSIDE the home or office where they take on the symbolic role of sentinel protectors. The thorns serve as an effective countering force against *shar chi* entering the home or office. But when placed inside the home or office, these same thorns that should protect become themselves poison arrows creating s*har chi* that attack (rather than protect) the home

BONSAI PLANTS

Are suggestive of stunted growth, and for this reason do not represent good feng shui. I am not referring to artistically pruned shrubs and plants. These bring great good energy to the home and office.

I am, instead, referring to varieties of large trees that have been cleverly and artificially <u>stunted</u> over many years, and are usually worth a great deal of money. Genuine Bonsai plants are extremely valuable, and also very pretty and irresistible. But they are not good feng shui as they signify blocks to one's growth. They are thus harmful to business feng shui.

If you have a passion for BONSAI and absolutely must have them in your home or garden. I strongly suggest you avoid placing them in the wood corners of the home or garden. This means the East or the Southeast. Placed in the North, they cause the least harm.

CHAPTER
ONE

FENG SHUI
IN THE
HOME

Personalized
Interior
Decoration

Hang feng shui <u>coins</u> or <u>bells</u> on doors | TIP 23

This is one of my personal favourite things to do to attract auspicious money luck into my home. As a result everyone living in my home benefits. Including the maid and gardener. I hang three Chinese coins on the door handles of my main doors – the kind that have the square holes in the center – tied together with red string which activates the essence of good fortune symbolized by the coins. The coins hang on the <u>INSIDE</u> of my doors and are thus deemed to be already inside my home !

Another good tip is to hang a small bell also on the door handle. But the bell should be hung OUTSIDE the door. This represents the bell attracting prosperity luck to flow towards the home. The bell is different from the coin. Its sound is believed to entice good fortune luck to come to the home. The coin represents wealth that has already come into the home.

Hang coins here on this door handle on the INSIDE

Hang a bell on your door handle but this time on the OUTSIDE of the door.

In following this tip there is no necessity to go overboard. You do not need to hang these coins on every single door in your home and indeed, whenever you over do any feng shui recommendation, the results can often turn from positive to negative. Never forget that feng shui is about balance. So limit the application of this tip to your main front door.

You should never hang any coins or other feng shui-energizing symbol on the back door. In feng shui the back door represents the way out for you. It takes care of protecting you and it is important from that perspective. To create good fortune feng shui it is sufficient to focus on the main front door.

This tip is particularly potent when your main front door happens to be located in the West or Northwest of your home. This is because both the coins and the bell symbolize the metal, the element of these two directions.

CHAPTER
ONE

FENG SHUI
IN
THE HOME

Placement
of
Household
Items

PROTECT THE FAMILY'S RICE URN

TIP 24

The Chinese bend backwards to take good care of their rice urn. This is because the urn symbolizes the rise or fall of the family's fortunes, Rice being the staple food of the Chinese, it represents everything to do with livelihoods, business and careers. Thus Chinese keep their rice in urns that have been passed down from their forefathers. This ensures continuity, and if the family is a wealthy family, the rice urn becomes an important symbol of the family's continued prosperity.

The rice urn is usually "inherited" by the family of the eldest son, and in the old days, the eldest daughter in law would go to great pains to ensure her family gets it. The rice urn is also kept hidden away in a storeroom. This implies that the family's wealth is safely hidden away. Embedded under the rice, there is usually a carefully wrapped red packet containing money in the form of coins. This red packet gets renewed each lunar New Year, and this ritual is on eof the most important rituals that have to be done on the eve of the first day of New Year. Again this ensures continuity of good fortune.

Usually if the preceding year has, on balance, been a good year, some coins from the previous year's red packet is added to the new one. If the past year had been one of difficulty, none of the old coins are added to the new red packet.

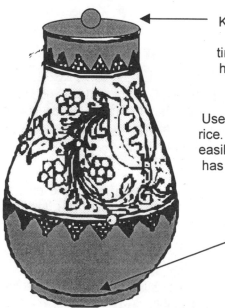

Keep the rice urn closed at all times, and keep it hidden away in a store room.

Use a strong container to keep your rice. Not something that gets broken easily. If you can, choose an urn that has auspicious symbols painted on.

Keep a red packet with money under the rice

CHAPTER
ONE

FENG SHUI
IN
THE HOME

Placement
of
Household
Items

Watch the position of your Cooker | TIP 25

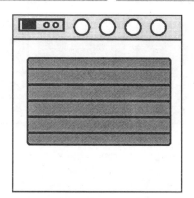

Many Compass school methods of feng shui strongly warn against the family's stove (or cooker) being placed in the NORTHWEST of the kitchen or the home. To be on the safe side I advise against having the kitchen in the Northwest, but if your kitchen is placed there, then you must at least make certain your stove/cooker is NOT in the Northwest corner of your kitchen. Why is this so ?

This recommendation is because the Northwest is the corner that is said to represent the Patriarch or breadwinner. If you place the cooker there you are burning the luck of the Patriarch and there can be nothing worse than destroying the luck of the family breadwinner.

The Northwest is also the corner that represents "heaven" so having the cooker or stove here suggests " *fire at heaven's gate*". And there is nothing more inauspicious than this. It is said that having the stove in this part of the kitchen causes the family's wealth to be wasted at worst. And that at best it causes the Hosui to get completely razed to the ground. Thus this is a serious feng shui defect which should be corrected. Remember that the stove represents the fire element, which is the only element capable of destroying the metal element of the northwest.

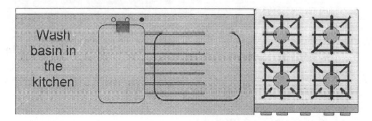

Wash basin in the kitchen

The second major point about kitchen arrangements is to watch out for the clash between the fire (stove/oven/cookers) and the water (refrigerator, dishwasher and sink) elements. These two elements should neither be placed next to each other, Nor should they be placed directly confronting each other. This latter arrangement has the water directly opposite the fire !
The direct confrontation orientation is more harmful than having the two elements side by side, and ovens do less harm than open fires.

CHAPTER
ONE

FENG SHUI
IN
THE HOME

Placement
of
Household
items

Place hi fi equipment along the West wall | TIP 26

Hi fi equipment signifies the metal element, which is excellent for the West sector of the living room

All stereo and hi fi equipment bring extra good luck to the house when placed against the West wall of the living room. Stereo sets placed in the West create the potential for huge good fortune that will ripen starting from the year 2003. The good fortune will last for twenty years

MIRRORS
and where to place them

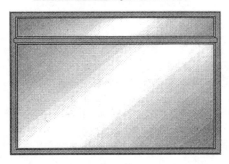

In feng shui, mirrors can be great energizers OR they can create big disasters. In the dining and living rooms mirrors are excellent. Create a mirror wall on the North side of the dining room to '*double*' the food of the family. Placing it in the North energizes the essence of protection for the household's livelihood, assuring the family of continued well being. It does not guarantee wealth and riches but it ensures the family will never lack for sustenance.
<u>Mirrors are a major taboo in the bedroom.</u> Here mirrors cause havoc in a couple's marriage and love life.

 Keep your television sets in the living room or family room. If you have a TV in your bedroom cover it with a cloth before you go to sleep. A television set directly facing the bed creates extreme *bad chi* for the couple and causes husband and wife, or lovers to be separated for long periods of time. Television sets facing the bed are similar to the effect of mirrors. Misfortune that creates severe unhappiness can result.

Mirrors are often responsible for the entrée of third parties into an otherwise good relationship. If you must have a mirror in your bedroom, keep them closed, or covered during the hours of sleep, and on no account let the mirror reflect the bed. And no mirrors on the ceiling please !

CHAPTER
ONE

FENG SHUI
IN
THE HOME

Placement
of
Household
Items

Dissolve the *shar chi* of open shelves | TIP 27

Open bookshelves resemble knives that send out "*shar chi*" or killing breath into the room. Whether these shelves are in your home or your office, my advice is to dissolve the *shar chi* created by putting doors onto your book cabinets. The effect of open shelves may not be felt immediately but residents of rooms with open shelves almost always succumb eventually by contracting illnesses that can prove fatal.

I have seen many large offices of corporate bosses where the shelves have been placed on three sides of the room to make the room fit into the interior decorator's idea of what an important corporate office should look like. I can only say that such shelves can cause the occupant of the room to succumb to a heart attack. Sad to say I have seen this borne out is several instances.

The exposed shelves resemble knives cutting into you

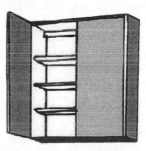

Close exposed book shelves with doors.

In circumstances where you really cannot do anything about the exposed shelves in your office or room, the next best thing to do is to arrange your books to 'flush" with the blades of the shelves so the effect created is to symbolically make the shelves disappear. This can be done with books and with large files.

It is not possible to use this method for shelves used to display decorative items. In this situation you might want to sandpaper the edges of the shelves. This in effect "blunts" the cutting sharpness of the shelves and does alleviate the situation somewhat.

Finally it might be useful to note that glass shelves are particularly harmful in the North corners while wooden shelves are harmful in the Southwest, the Northeast as well as the center of any room. Plastic shelves are the least harmful of all.

CHAPTER
ONE

FENG SHUI
IN
THE HOME

Placement
of
Household
Items

Do not over decorate your toilets

TIP 28

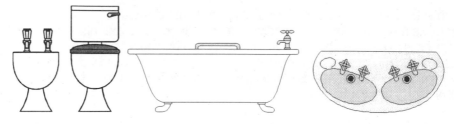

Ever since I became an avid fan of feng shui, I have strenuously warned my wealthy friends against spending too much money making the toilets and bathrooms of their home their pride and joy. It is very easy to succumb to this preoccupation with the toilet and end up over decorating a part of the home that has the greatest potential of creating havoc with your feng shui.

Toilet and bathroom fittings are horrendously expensive. yet many people like their toilets and bathroom very large. A big mistake, because toilets create bad feng shui in whatever every corner they are located. The actual type of bad luck depends on which corner is "*afflicted*. Chinese homes of a long ago age rarely had toilets. Night soil carriers carried away the family's waste material. The rich had their baths brought in by servants. And even poor peasants had their toilets built some way away from the home.

For modern living I advise toilets to be made small, hidden away and always kept closed. It is also not necessary to decorate the toilet with paintings, flowers, antique spots and other toilet paraphernalia. Do not place auspicious flowers and symbols in the toilet as this can sometimes cause severe problems in the area of life which you desperately wish to correct.

Let me tell you a story. I had a friend whose toilet was located in the *children's corner*. Her children's grades suffered and they endured one disappointment after another. Nothing they did could succeed. I told her to place a mirror on the toilet door to make the toilet symbolically disappear. This worked. Both the children graduated with excellent grades. Both found good jobs. And then my friend started to place flowers in her toilet – fake peonies and plum blossoms - to apparently *energize* her children's corner. She forgot she was energizing her toilet. The peonies were to bring romance luck to her daughter.
Her daughter did find romance and love but with a good for nothing boy who brought nothing but heartache to the family. It was only after the toilet was completely cleared of the flowers that her daughter came to her senses and discarded the objectionable young man. Be careful !

CHAPTER
ONE

FENG SHUI
IN
THE HOME

Placement
of
Household
Items

Keep brooms and mops out of sight | TIP 29

Mops and brooms are associated with the "sweeping " out of the negative and stale energy of the home. But brooms can also sweep away good and auspicious energy. As such, feng shui advises they be kept out of sight after the action of cleaning is done.

You will never see brooms, mops and other cleaning paraphernalia in traditional Chinese home, especially those homes where the matriarch is very strong. Those of the older generation who grew up on a diet of cultural superstition consider it extremely inauspicious to see brooms around the home instead of being kept away. Exposed brooms are especially forbidden in dining rooms. The presence of exposed brooms here will *"sweep away the family's rice bowl and livelihood."* And is thus considered as bad feng shui.

Thus brooms and mops should be kept hidden away in back closets. This guideline should also be followed with electric cleaners as well.

A feng shui tip to keep out intruders and burglars

Here is an unusual tip passed on to me years ago by someone in Hong Kong. In the early years of my nine year stay in Hong Kong I was paranoid about security, and went to elaborate pains to install burglar alarm systems, except these super sensitive installations often led to false alarms and embarrassing moments with the local police. in the middle of the night.

I was thus advised by a feng shui consultant, who happened to be the father of one of my own bank employees that the best way to keep intruders away was to lean a broom <u>upside down</u> against the wall and facing the front door. This would keep out unwanted visitors. If you want to use this tip, place the broom outside the home, not on the inside. Keep the broom there during the nocturnal hours. In the daytime keep the broom out of sight !

CHAPTER
TWO

FENG SHUI
IN ALL YOUR
RELATION
SHIPS

ENHANCING
FAMILY
HAPPINESS

A family room in the center for HARMONY	TIP 30

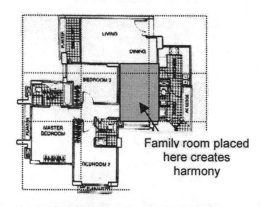

Family room placed
here creates
harmony

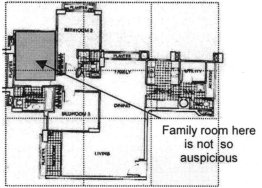

Family room here
is not so
auspicious

This tip has to do with the placement of rooms in the overall layout plan of your home. If you examine the layout plans of the two houses on the left you will note that the family rooms of the two houses are in different locations. The family room in the first house is in the center and is thus more conducive to family harmony than the location of the family room in the second plan. The dotted lines are the imaginary lines of a *Lo Shu* square superimposed on the layout plan.

A *Lo Shu* square is a nine sector grid which is used as a feng shui tool that enables analysis to be undertaken.

What NOT to have in the center !

A staircase in the center is BAD ! If the staircase is spiral it is very bad as this "bores' into the heart of the home. If placed in the center, curved or straight staircases are not as damaging as spiral staircases. If you have a center staircase do not carpet in red or green.

Kitchens and bedrooms should not be in the center of the home since these lay undue importance on eating and sleeping. A kitchen in the center presses down on the entire family's good fortune. You should relocate the kitchen if you have this kind of layout.

In this case we are using the Lo Shu square help in determining the center of the home. It is very easy to see if the family room is in the center grid of the Lo Shu. If so, the room is auspicious for the family, There will be goodwill amongst family members. Husband and wife stay on good terms.

Children will tend to be more obedient and siblings stay close to each other.

CHAPTER
TWO

FENG SHUI
IN ALL YOUR
RELATION
SHIPS

ENHANCING
FAMILY
HAPPINESS

Happy family portraits bring togetherness | TIP 31

One of the best and most effective methods of creating a sense of family togetherness is to hang a large family portrait in a place of honor in the living room or family room.

Every member of the family should be included in the portrait, and to symbolize happiness, every member should be smiling. Arrange the members of the family in a way that creates a shape most suitable to the element of the family patriarch.

<u>Triangular arrangement:</u>
If you choose this arrangement, make sure the bread winner OR family patriarch is placed at the apex of the triangle. This particular arrangement creates the element of fire, and it also signifies the precious *yang* energy. This arrangement is particularly excellent when the patriarch is born in a <u>fire</u> or <u>earth</u> year. I used this arrangement for our family portrait shown here.

<u>A wavy arrangement</u>
This arrangement creates the water element. It is a yin shape and would be great if there is excessive yang energy in the home. The patriarch or bread winner should be in the center, and the heads of the people in the picture are not level thereby creating a wavy shape. This is excellent when the patriarch was born in a <u>water</u> or <u>wood</u> year.

<u>A Rectangular arrangement</u>
This arrangement suggests the <u>wood</u> element, and is probably the most common. Here, all members pose in a way that has everyone's head level. The arrangement also suggests a regular and balanced shape. This arrangement is suitable where the Patriarch is born in a wood or fire year.

<u>Square arrangement</u>
This is similar to the rectangle and is especially suited for small families. For instance, four in a picture makes a perfect square, a shape that suggests the <u>earth</u> element.

This arrangement is suitable for everyone since the earth element also signifies the family. It is especially excellent if the Patriarch was born in a <u>metal</u> year since earth produces metal in the cycle of the elements.

CHAPTER
TWO

FENG SHUI
IN ALL YOUR
RELATION
SHIPS

ENHANCING
FAMILY
HAPPINESS

Mandarin ducks to enhance your love life | TIP 32

Mandarin ducks are to feng shui what lovebirds are to the West. You will find these ducks are depicted in many items of the Chinese arts and crafts. This is because a pair mandarin ducks is regarded as a symbol of romance, love and fidelity for young couples.

Placed in the Southwest corners of bedrooms or of the home these ducks create energies that greatly enhance your love life. If you are single, hang a painting of these ducks, or get a pair of carved wooden ducks from the Chinese emporium and place them in your bedroom. Make sure you put a pair, not one or three since the connotation of one is that you will stay stubbornly single, and that of three implies a marriage or love relationship that could well get crowded! Also, do make certain that you place a male and a female in the pair – not two males or two females. Please ask the shop assistant to tell you the difference between the male duck and the female duck.

If you are not able to find the mandarin duck, please use the modern equivalent of the lovebird, but again make sure you display a pair. This can be in the form of a painting, or a picture. Do not keep the real thing. I must hasten to say that as a general rule I discourage keeping birds in cages as I regard this as <u>bad</u> feng shui. It symbolizes an inability to "fly" i.e. to grow one's ambitions.

CHAPTER
TWO

FENG SHUI
IN ALL YOUR
RELATIONSHIPS

ENHANCING
FAMILY
HAPPINESS

Mirrors in the bedroom cause problems | TIP 33

mirrors

A cabinet with so many mirrors should
NOT be placed in the bedroom

Mirrors possess a special form of energy, which can be either very good or very bad. The one place where mirrors can do a great deal of harm is the bedroom,

One should be very careful about mirrors that directly face the bed. This happens when built in cupboards have mirror doors that directly reflect the bed. Feng shui masters attribute the breakdown of marriages, and especially, infidelity, to the negative effect of mirrors reflecting the bed. In feng shui lore the reason given is that the mirror creates energies which disturb the relationship of the sleeping couple.

Feng shui master, Mr. Yap also warn against mirrors, He maintains that the shock of suddenly seeing oneself reflected in the mirror upon waking up, can be so disturbing that negative energies get created for the person.

Mr. Yap once described the ritual of "spiritually cleansing" a place believed haunted or disturbed by wandering spirits. The ritual involves the use of a mirror to "reflect" the spirit(s) into the mirror, after which the mirror itself would be blessed in order to control the bad spirits. If this part of the ritual is not done properly, Mr. Yap told me, the spirits stay trapped inside the mirror. Since hearing that sinister tale, I have been extra careful with mirrors.
Because the bedroom is the room we occupy during the nocturnal hours I prefer not to have mirrors anywhere near or reflecting me. Far better to keep the mirrors out of sight when I sleep and am vulnerable.

CHAPTER
TWO

FENG SHUI
IN ALL YOUR
RELATION
SHIPS

ENHANCING
FAMILY
HAPPINESS

Separate mattresses lead to separation | TIP 34

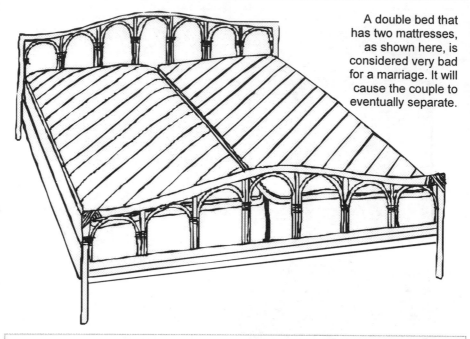

A double bed that has two mattresses, as shown here, is considered very bad for a marriage. It will cause the couple to eventually separate.

If you want to take feng shui into consideration when planning your Master bedroom, then you should make certain your double bed is REALLY a double bed and that you have a single piece of mattress. You should never have two mattresses as shown above since this symbolically creates a schism between the sleeping couple. It is far better to have two separate beds, or even have separate bedrooms to take account of two people having different auspicious directions than to sleep on a bed with two mattresses.

Two other features that can cause the couple to split or have severe misunderstandings that lead to separation are:

1. When there is a beam directly above the bed that symbolically splits the bed into two. If your bed is situated directly below such a beam (which is a bad configuration anyway) do try to move the bed out from under it. If you cannot do this then create a false ceiling that makes the beam symbolically *disappear.*
2. When the bed lies between two doors that create an imaginary line that cuts the bed into two ... this is a very inauspicious arrangement anyway, and you should either move the bed, or place a screen to block out one of the doors.

CHAPTER
TWO

FENG SHUI
IN ALL YOUR
RELATIONSHIPS

ENHANCING
FAMILY
HAPPINESS

Don't sleep facing the door | TIP 35

The death position is when one has one's feet are directly facing the door. The corpses of dead relatives are placed this way - with the feet directly pointed towards the door - prior to the funeral. This arrangement is deemed to be a very excellent *yin* position for the dead. But it is deadly for the living !

Actually Feng shui advises that neither the head nor the feet should be pointed directly at the door of the room. Thus when positioning the bed, it is always advisable to have it placed either to the left or right of the door.

If there is an attached or ensuite bathroom/toilet, it is important to make certain that the two doors, ie the entrance door, and the toilet door, are not aligned in a straight line. Worse, if the bed itself is sandwiched in between. If yours is such a situation it calls for severe measures to be taken. Place a screen or cabinet to block off one of the doors,

And move the bed but in so doing, do not end up having the bed pointed to either the toilet door or the entrance door. If your bedroom is very small and you have no choice then I advise you to place your bed with the headboard at one of the corners. This sort of irregular arrangement is acceptable.

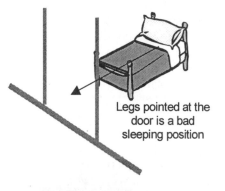
Legs pointed at the door is a bad sleeping position

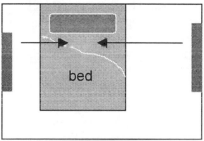
If your bed lies between two doors as shown here, try to block one of the doors with a screen

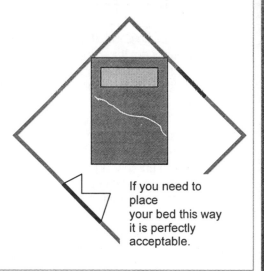
If you need to place your bed this way it is perfectly acceptable.

CHAPTER
TWO

FENG SHUI
IN ALL
YOUR
RELATION
SHIPS

ENHANCING
FAMILY
HAPPINESS

A few tips for childless couples

TIP 36

One reason I am so enamoured of feng shui is that it really can bring enormous happiness to one's life, especially when it involves making one's family life happier and more meaningful. It is especially effective in helping couples who want children but seem to be having a hard time conceiving. I am not referring to those with medical problems. I am saying that if you have tried and checked everything and find there is nothing wrong with you, or your partner, and still you cannot conceive, then feng shui might be able to help. This was what happened to me.

My inability to conceive had been due to a huge poison arrow which took the form of a large casuarina tree not ten feet from my main door. This created bad *shar chi* that hit my front door. We were childless for nine years ! If you are having a hard time conceiving, it is a good idea to check whether anything sharp, pointed or threatening is hurting your main door OR your bed ! Chances are you will find something and when you do try to shield it or block it off from view. OR move out like we did. We moved to another house and we designed our new home according to feng shui principles, concentrating on activating our descendants luck. What we did is sketched out here.

Firstly

Please check the husband's *nien yen* direction based on the Table given on page 2. Then try to occupy the bedroom that is located in his *nien yen* location. Next, position the bed so you both sleep in his *nien yen* direction. This activates his descendents luck.

In feng shui the effect of the women's descendents luck is not counted.

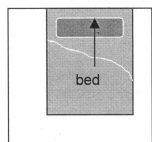

The arrow should be pointed to the man's *nien yen* direction

Secondly,

Look for a painting or picture of children, and hang it in the vicinity of the bed. In the imperial palaces of the Forbidden city, the emperor's conjugal bed is decorated with screens and embroidery of the famous *"100 children"* to symbolize great fertility in his encounters with his many wives.

Thirdly,

Find young virgin born in the year of the dragon and ask him to symbolically *"roll"* across your bed. Ideally this should have been done on the wedding night, but better late than never. Or place a small representation of the dragon next to the bed to simulate precious yang energy.

CHAPTER
TWO

FENG SHUI
IN ALL YOUR
RELATIONSHIPS

ENHANCING
FAMILY
HAPPINESS

Coping with children difficulties | TIP 37

If you are having problems with your children, you must check the feng shui of your home. First you should walk through your house and investigate whether anything, any structure or object may be harming your front door OR the beds and desks of your children. See if the door into the children's room is directly facing a toilet or a staircase. The negative energy created can cause the resident to feel listless, rebellious and completely lacking in motivation. Good *yang* energy is depleted. Try to change rooms for your child OR hang a small windchime above the door between the door and the staircase or toilet.

If your problem is a teenager who is disobedient, who does not like coming home and who seems to have no sensitivity to the family then you MUST investigate his or her sleeping direction. Check the KUA number and try to make him/her sleep with the head pointed to the *nien yen* direction. This is a family oriented direction and will make a great deal of difference. Just using this one tip we have helped a great many of our friends with their rebellious teenagers.

Try also to dissuade your son or daughter from sleeping on the floor, or on a bed so low as to be level to the floor. This is neither auspicious nor conducive to his/her personal happiness. Instead the mind will be disturbed and there will also be the possibility of problems with health.

If you let your baby sit at the corner edge of the table baby will get hit by poison arrow !

Check the direction your son is facing when he works. Let him face his *Fu wei* direction if you want his grades at school to improve

When the problem with your children has to do with study grades, their work could be suffering because of wrong sitting direction. For children, the direction to tap is their respective *fu wei* direction. Check what these directions are based on date of birth from page 2; then let your child sleep with his/her head pointed in the *fu wei* and work at the desk facing the *fu wei* direction.

Next hang, or place a small crystal in the Northeast corner of the bedroom. The crystal is an excellent educational energizer that harmonizes very well with the NE, which is also the education corner.

CHAPTER
TWO

FENG SHUI
IN ALL YOUR
RELATION
SHIPS

ENHANCING
YOUR
LOVE LIFE

Attract romance and love with crystals | TIP 38

A cluster of natural quartz crystals is extremely effective for activating the earth energies of the SW corner. This attracts romance into your life

**Man made crystals like the one shown above can also be used, and are especially effective when placed by a sunny window sill.
This catches the sunlight and brings in wonderful yang energy from the sunlight. It is a very auspicious way of using crystals.**

The power of crystals can be used in the practice of feng shui. Natural crystals are especially effective for energizing the Southwest corner of your bedroom or living room. Crystals are one of the best symbols of "*mother earth*" and the SW is the corner of big earth. The Southwest is also the corner that governs the luck of love, romance and family happiness.

This is applicable for everyone irrespective of your particular KUA number. If you activate the Southwest corner of your bedroom you will have greater harmony and happiness in all your relationships with loved ones. If you do it in the living room, everyone living in your home benefits. Before you display the crystal, wash it thoroughly to get rid of any negative energies it may be carrying. Do this by soaking it in sea salt water for seven days and seven nights.

CHAPTER
TWO

FENG SHUI
IN ALL YOUR
RELATION
SHIPS

ENHANCING
YOUR
LOVE LIFE

Get him/her to commit with feng shui | TIP 39

Strengthen the SW corner with lights.
If your problem is getting your partner to make a commitment, to propose
marriage, or simply to acknowledge you are an "*item*" then, in addition to
displaying a crystal in the Southwest corner of love, you should give strength to
the crystal by installing a very bright light there. The best feng shui energizer for
this purpose if to hang a crystal chandelier in the Southwest corner, but any
bright light, kept turned on for at least 3 hours every night would be helpful. It is
unnecessary to overdo things by making the light too bright. Halogens and
spotlights are much too harsh, and are not good feng shui,

Problem could be the toilet
Sometimes the problem is created by the presence of a toilet in the Southwest
corner of the home. I have seen so many examples of this being the cause of
my friends' children having a hard time getting married even though they were
not lacking in suitors. If you have a toilet in the SW that is spoiling your chances
of getting married, my suggestion is for you to keep the toilet permanently
locked. Stop using the toilet altogether and turn it into a store room. If you
cannot do this, the next best thing is to hand *a five rod windchime that is made
of wood and is painted black or brown* to "press down on the bad energy being
created by the toilet. Another way of making the toilet '*disappear*' is to hang a
full-length mirror on the door of the toilet.

The "*Moutan*" flower of peony can be
helpful to women who are keen to settle
down. Hang a fan with peony flowers in
your bedroom. This will vastly improve
your chances of finding someone willing
to settle down with you.

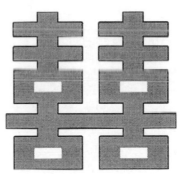

Another good way to activate
the wedding luck of people of
marriageable age is to place a
few large boulders in the SW
corner of the garden. Paint the
double happiness symbol in
red on the rock, OR tie red
string around the rock to
activate its inherent energies.

39

CHAPTER
TWO

FENG SHUI
IN ALL YOUR
RELATION
SHIPS

ENHANCING
YOUR
LOVE LIFE

Energizing your love corners | TIP 40

In addition to the general feng shui tips on love and romance, you can also energize and protect your personalized *"nien yen" direction* and location. Check your personal *nien yen* direction from page 2; then try to get at least 3 of the following to describe your personal space. It is never possible to get everything correctly aligned to suit your personalized direction. Thus as long as you get about 60 to 70% right, your feng shui will work in your favour.

1.   Sleep with your head pointed to your *nien yen*
2.   Choose a bedroom which is in your *nien yen* corner
3.   Make sure your toilet is NOT in your *nien yen.*
4.   Let your bedroom door face your *nien yen* direction
5.   Make sure your *nien yen* corner is not missing

If your nien yen is South,
Hang a bright light in the South corner of your bedroom. Then place a small red light in the Northwest corner, and hang a windchime in the Northeast.
If your nien yen is Northwest,
Place a crystal in the Northwest corner of your bedroom. Then put a piece of furniture painted black in the South, and a metal windchime in the Southeast.
If your nien yen is Southeast
Place a small red light in the Southeast of your bedroom. Then hang a windchime in the Northeast and place another red light in the Northwest.
If your nien yen is East
Place a small red light in the East. Then decorate the West of your bedroom with something red, and the Southwest corner with something black.
If your nien yen is Northwest
Place a silver picture frame in the Northwest. Then decorate the east and Southeast in metallic or gray colors.
If your nien yen is Southwest
Place a red light or crystals in the Southwest of your bedroom. Place crystals in the North corner and decorate the East corner in metallic colors.
If your nein yen is Northeast
Place a red light or crystals in the Northeast and decorate the East and Southeast of your bedroom in metallic or gray colors.
If your nien yen is West
Have a golden or silver collared bedspread and hang a silver-framed photo in the West wall of the bedroom. Then place crystals in the North corner.
If your nien yen is in the North
Display something small that is painted black in the North part of your bedroom. Then decorate the West and Southwest in metallic or gray colors.

CHAPTER
TWO

FENG SHUI
IN ALL
YOUR
RELATION
SHIPS

ENHANCING
YOUR
LOVE LIFE

Beware exclusively male/female energies | TIP 41

A passionately professional girlfriend of mine had a huge reproduction of the famous Chinese painting entitled *"One hundred beauties of Suchou"* a classic painting commissioned by the Ching Emperor *Chien Lung*, centuries ago in celebration of the beautiful women of Suchou. This beautiful painting, rendered in silk hung in her living room. Sue had so many women in her life, and so many girlfriends many wondered if she was "that way inclined". I wondered too, until she confided to me one day that nothing would make her happier than to get married and raise a family. " *But I don't seem to be able to keep any relationship going for longer than two months"* she laughed. Then going on 38 years old, she admitted she was getting desperate. I checked her *nien yen* and told her about feng shui.

I persuaded her to give away her *100 Beauties* painting explaining that the female yin energies created by all those women in that painting was much too powerful. She balked at first but later presented it to her brother as a birthday gift.

Shortly thereafter, she met Brian who proposed after a three month courtship. Today eleven years later, they are still happily married.

If you want to find a partner; if you wish to get married; if you want the happiness of romance and family life; if you really do not want to be alone, then the first thing to do is go round your home and see if you are displaying anything that symbolize a SINGLE gender. If you are a woman, see if your paintings are all of women. If you hang nothing but females on all the walls of your home, it is unlikely your home can attract the "male" energy. This situation is not as surprising as it seems. I have visited enough single girlfriends *'bachelor pads'* to find nothing but beautiful paintings of women on their walls. My girlfriends were not gay. Just art lovers who appreciated the female form and completely forgot to create balance in the display of their artwork.

I had another friend who had the same problem. Robert was a very nice iconoclastic English male bachelor – one of those investment-banking types really good at making money but quite hopeless with women. Robert lived alone in a stunning apartment on the Peak in Hong Kong. At one of the dinner parties he gave each time he found a new girlfriend to help him "play host", I noticed that his home had nothing but *"male type decorations"* There were pictures of cricket stars and paintings of naval heroes. There were Sotheby's type sculptures of men and busts of dead poets. There was nothing that suggested anything feminine. His home was completely too *"yang"* by far. When he confided he was having no luck with women, that I told him about the lack of female energy in his home. Robert changed this with two marvelous paintings of the female form. The resulting balance of energies has long since created a happy ending for Robert and his delightful wife Natalie.

CHAPTER
TWO

FENG SHUI
IN ALL YOUR
RELATION
SHIPS

ENHANCING
YOUR
LOVE LIFE

Keep things in pairs

TIP 42

If you don't like being alone and want someone to share your life with, you would be well advised to surround your personal space with things that symbolize Nature's uncontrived pairing of the *male* with the *female*. The ultimate symbol of Chinese feng shui is the yin/yang symbol (shown here) which encapsulates the complementarily of the male/female union. This represents the balance that is so vital in feng shui symbolism.

Left: The auspicious Double fish

Right: The Footsteps of Buddha

Above: A pair of butterflies is an unhappy symbol

Left: a pair of mandarin ducks spell happiness for young lovers.

The Chinese are extremely conscious of the auspiciousness of giving, taking or displaying things in pairs. Many of the prosperity and good luck symbols of the Chinese come in pairs the ultimate of which is of course the dragon. Dragons are either shown in pairs – two dragons frolicking with the eternal pearl, or a dragon and a phoenix to symbolize conjugal happiness.

Mandarin ducks, which symbolize the happiness of young love, are also always shown in pairs. Whether drawn onto ceramics or as brush paintings, they are NEVER featured alone. Neither will there be three in a painting. Another symbol of love is a pair of butterflies although this is seldom recommended since this is a symbol of love that ends in tragedy. The folk tale of the star crossed lovers who die in each other's arms and are reunited as butterflies is a well known one. Even this symbol of tragic love is shown as a pair.

Two other extremely meaningful and auspicious symbols are the double fish, which is a very lucky symbol and the pair of footsteps which signify Buddha's footsteps. This is also a religious symbol for Buddhists of all traditions, and it expresses the karmic happiness of prosperous rebirths after death.

CHAPTER
TWO

FENG SHUI
IN ALL YOUR
RELATION
SHIPS

ENHANCING
YOUR
LOVE LIFE

Happiness decor for the bedroom | TIP 43

The conventional feng shui advice for bedrooms is that since it is a place of rest. Colors should be more suggestive of *yin,* rather than *yang* energies, although never to such an extent that excessiveness causes imbalance.

For happiness luck in one's love relationship however, feng shui does prescribe the use of warmer, *yang* colors. In the old days this was usually related to fertility energizers to create descendants luck. Indeed, the Chinese preoccupation with fertility in marriages, and conjugal performance of the male has spawned all kinds of aphrodisiacs and symbols that supposedly create descendants' luck and reproductive performance. There are even different types of potions as well as supposedly "*auspicious times*" to make love to ensure that any baby conceived is a male rather than a female child.

We can borrow from the list of recommendations given to young couples to ensure they have a happy love life. Here are some do's and don'ts that were passed to me by the older female members of my extended family.

1. Decorate the bedroom in red during the early years of marriage. If red is found to be too strong, use pink or peach. Red creates passion and a great deal of yang energy which brings good fortune to the union. White is a good color for bedsheets, but do not use blue sheets. Blue carpets and wallpaper are fine.
2. Never put live plants and flowers in the bedroom; but fruits are excellent especially the pomegranate which is a symbol of fertility.
3. Paintings hung in the rooms of married couples should preferably feature children and ripe fruits signifying the happy result of their pairing. Flowers should be avoided. Once married, remove the painting of the peony since this only creates the danger of additional wives. In the old days men could happily take on concubines. In today's world, the entrée of a sweet young thing into the marriage is NOT considered good feng shui. So better to keep the peony painting in the store room until your own daughters reach marriageable age and can benefit from its romantic vibes !
4. Place small red lights to energize passion and fertility.
5. Avoid anything that suggests water. Do not have an aquarium or a basin in your bedroom. It causes misunderstandings and sleepless nights. A flask or a glass of water is fine but NOT a painting of a lake or a waterfall!
6. In the old days, wealthy families had the double happiness symbol carved as elaborate designs into their bedroom furniture. You can also display this very auspicious symbol in your bedroom. This symbol is on page 39. Use your own creativity to see how you can incorporate it into your bedroom design.

CHAPTER
TWO

FENG SHUI
IN ALL YOUR
RELATION
SHIPS

ENHANCING
YOUR
LOVE LIFE

Get help from "mother earth"

TIP 44

In feng shui when we speak of mother earth, we think of the whole practice itself. Feng shui refers to the luck of the earth., and the earth element takes on significance because of this. Symbolically, the direction SOUTHWEST and the trigram KUN (three broken lines) represent mother earth.

A feng shui Master I met in Hong Kong once told me that there were three hexagrams in the I Ching' that could be effectively harnessed to create different types of good fortune for the home. I had been advised that this gentleman was particularly well schooled in the I Ching and its interpretation for divinitive purposes, and that he was also knowledgeable about feng shui. He did not speak English, but I was fascinated with the way he explained the influence of each of the sixty-four hexagrams in the home. The three hexagrams he claimed could be effectively energized for the home were the hexagrams *Kun, CHien* and *Sheng.*

For happiness in relationships and love, and especially to foster family harmony he recommended that help be obtained from *mother earth* by displaying the hexagram Kun (which is created by doubling the three broken lines thereby creating six broken lines) in the Southwest corner of the home. This, he said would strengthen the energies of the matriarch

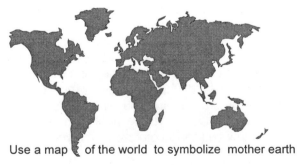

Use a map of the world to symbolize mother earth

The Trigram KUN , which rules the SOUTHWEST symbolizes Mother Earth – big earth. It is the ultimate yin trigram, and it personifies the female energy in all of us. It is possible to draw on the energies of the KUN trigram to enhance one's love life.

The trigram *Kun* is also excellent for promoting family harmony and drawing on the strength of the female maternal energies of the household.

A third use of this trigram is as formidable support for the family Patriarch.

The trigram KUN enhances the Trigram CHIEN of the Northwest. Both of these trigrams can be *doubled* to be transformed into hexagrams of the same name. Thus the hexagram KUN is regarded as mother earth doubled, made up of six broken lines, the *ultimate yin* hexagram; while the hexagram CHIEN is The male patriarch doubled, made up of six unbroken lines – the *ultimate yang* hexagram.

CHAPTER
TWO

FENG SHUI
IN ALL YOUR
RELATIONSHIPS

ENHANCING
YOUR
LOVE LIFE

Hang a chandelier in the Southwest | TIP 45

I am a great fan of chandeliers and use it lavishly to energize different types of good fortune *chi* in my own home. I hang a small one just outside my front door to seduce in the good *chi*, and I hang a slightly larger one in the foyer inside the main door to attract the *chi* to enter into my home. Then I hang a really large one above my dining table to symbolize precious *yang* energy for the food on the table.

But the most spectacular use of the chandelier is in the Southwest of the home – where the combination <u>of fire and earth</u> brings wonderful love luck to every resident member. Married couples will be far happier with each other while younger members will never be short of boyfriends or girlfriends!

The chandelier in the Southwest is an excellent activator of relationship luck. It makes residents popular with friends and family alike, and it also creates greater harmony within the home, thereby reducing friction between spouses and rivalry between siblings. Try to hang the chandelier in the Southwest of the home, rather than the Southwest of a single room.

CHAPTER
TWO

FENG SHUI
IN
ALL YOUR
RELATION
SHIPS

ENHANCING
FRIENDSHIPS

BOOST SOCIAL LIFE with FENG SHUI | TIP 46

The best way to create the kind of luck that brings an active social life is to use bright lights to give a boost of yang energy to the SOUTHWEST corner of your home. There are many ways to do this. The best method is to light up the Southwest part of your garden with a very bright garden light. The placement of lights just outside the home, but within your compound attracts the precious mother energy of the Southwest into the vicinity of your home. The way I activate this aspect of my luck is that I place three round lights (like the type shown on the right) above a pole placed about five feet above the ground. This is better than lighting from below. I also make sure that the rod holding the lights is hollow since this encourages earth energy to rise; Since the Southwest is the place of big earth in terms of the five elements this creates excellent energy.

ground

For those living in apartments

If you do not have a Southwestern part to your garden, or if you live in an apartment, it is a good idea to install a similar light if you have a balcony or terrace in the Southwest. Those with roof gardens can also use the same method of activating the southwest part of the roof garden. If you like you can also use *two* lamps instead of three since two is the number associated with the Southwest.

If all you have to work with is a small apartment – a living room and a bedroom – then the thing to do is to energize the living room. Identify the Southwest of your home with a compass. The corner, which is marked Southwest on your compass, is the Southwest. This corner is NOT determined by the location of your front door.

Place a stand lamp in that corner. Make it red, a bright yellow or orange if you wish to strengthen the symbolism of *yang* energy. Such a lamp should not be so large as to dominate the room, but it should also not be too small. If you like you can place the lamp on a table. Whatever you do the lights should be at least five feet above the ground level. You can also hang a light in this corner. I hang crystal chandeliers in the Southwest corners of all my public rooms. Do not use this method for the bedroom !

CHAPTER
TWO

FENG SHUI
IN
ALL YOUR
RELATION
SHIPS

ENHANCING
FRIENDSHIPS

Windchimes to increase your popularity | TIP 47

There has been a great deal of contradictory recommendations regarding the use of windchimes as a feng shui-enhancing tool. It has even been suggested to me at several seminars of mine that hanging windchimes in the home could well attract wandering spirits who thus disturb the energies of the home. I want to say here categorically that windchimes are an excellent enhancing tool. They do not attract '*spirits*'. I have hung windchime in my home for over twenty years and they have brought me nothing but good luck and good fortune. The key to creating auspicious energy by hanging windchimes is to determine the following three things:

1. Whether you are using windchime made of wood, ceramic or metal. The material that your windchime is made of can enhance or destroy the element of the "corner" in which it is placed. Thus it is vital to get this right. To enhance energies of corners use windchimes according to the element of the corner. This means metal chimes are best for the West, Northwest, and North. Ceramic chimes are best for Southwest, Northeast and center. Wood chimes are best for East, Southeast and South.

2. The number of rods you have in your windchime. To enhance luck use 6,or 8 rods. To suppress bad luck use 5 rods.

3. Whether you are using windchimes to suppress the bad luck of a specific corner, or structure. Or whether you are using windchimes as a feng shui energizing and enhancing tool. If you use it to press down the bad luck caused by an offensive structure or poison arrow, then you should use a metal windchime with five rods.

To enhance your social popularity, hang either a two Or nine rod windchime made of either crystal or ceramics in the SOUTH-WEST corner of your living room. This is a feng shui enhancing method best implemented in the public areas of your home. Thus do not apply this method in the bedroom or the study. To attract influential people into your life, select a windchime with six or eight rods made of metal and hang it in the NORTHWESTERN part of the living room.

CHAPTER
TWO

FENG SHUI
IN
ALL YOUR
RELATION
SHIPS

ENHANCING
FRIENDSHIPS

Strengthen friendships with pine branches | TIP 48

I have discovered that the use of pine branches to *"cleanse"* homes of negative energy is used by certain Red Indian tribes of North America. In Tibet and Nepal, the dried leaves of pine trees are used to make pungent smelling incense which I was told were excellent for blessing abodes when used during prayer sessions, *pujas* or offerings to their deities.

In feng shui the pine tree is a popular and frequently used symbol of longevity, and is also associated with lifelong friendships.

If you want to use pine branches in feng shui, choose from local varieties in your place of residence. Christmas pines, junipers and any kind of cone shaped trees will do. Pluck a branch of pine. Choose a branch which has three sub branches to symbolize the three types of luck – heaven, earth and mankind luck. Then place the branch near the front of the main door. The foyer area will be excellent. Since this where the incoming chi enters the home. For it to meet with the auspicious symbol of pine leaves would be most beneficial.

In the old days martial arts exponents who regarded themselves as *blood brothers* would seal their undying bond to each other by rubbing their palms with the smoke of a fire started with the twigs and dried leaves of a pine tree. The ritual involved rubbing the palms over the fire as the smoke rises, and then rubbing each other's palms, before rubbing the face. This was believed to seal the friendship until death.

Place the pine branch in water for a maximum of three days or until the pine needles start to drop. In addition to strengthening friendships, this will also create excellent long life luck for residents, and is especially recommended in homes occupied by older people. To strengthen the longevity luck of the family patriarch pine branches can be placed in the Northwest corner of the living room. An alternative to using real pine leaves would be to hang a landscape painting of mountains filled with pine trees.

Any variety of pine tree is fine but the junipers are supposed to be the most potent for putting the seal on friendships.

CHAPTER
TWO

FENG SHUI
IN
ALL YOUR
RELATION
SHIPS

ENHANCING
FRIENDSHIPS

Avoid having three in a picture — TIP 49

Three in a picture is NOT recommended for friendships. But three in a picture does no harm if the picture is of family members. Indeed, <u>happy</u> family portraits spell excellent feng shui and for those of you with three member families (like me) the best feng shui method of taking pictures is to arrange yourself in a triangle, placing the most important member of the trio at the apex of the triangle. This is illustrated here in the two sketches below.

The Chinese are extremely superstitious about having three people in a picture. In the old days, artists are never allowed to paint three comrades in one picture. Even two in a picture was deemed unlucky. But three in a picture was believed to create the cause for conflict, or separation between those in the picture. The one in the middle would be separated from the two at the side. It is useful to keep this in mind when snapping pictures with your friends.

TIPS ON HANGING PICTURES IN THE HOME
1. Never hang photographs of family members directly facing a toilet.
2. Never hang your picture directly facing an inauspicious direction.
3. Never hang a family portrait directly facing the front door.
4. Never hang a family portrait directly facing a staircase.
5. Never hang family portraits in the basement.

CHAPTER
TWO

FENG SHUI
IN
ALL YOUR
RELATION
SHIPS

ENHANCING
FRIENDSHIPS

Seating friends at a dinner party | TIP 50

If you want your dinner parties to be successful social occasions, then in addition to applying the generally accepted tips on entertaining, you might want to consider using feng shui techniques for making sure everyone has a good time. The feel good factor can be easily put into practice by making certain that every guest of yours is seated according his/her most auspicious direction. Calculate their respective KUA numbers (from Page 2) and find out their most auspicious directions. Then seat each of them according to at least one of their respective four excellent directions. This will be a surefire guarantee that everyone will enjoy the evening. There will be harmony and excellent rapport between everyone.

The practice of placing guests of different genders next to each other is excellent for ensuring good yin and yang balance, but this is not as important as getting their directions right.

Round tables are always to be preferred over rectangular tables, but rectangular tables are better than T shaped or L shaped arrangements. If the number of guests coming for dinner exceeds the number of chairs you have available, it is better to make it a buffet dinner than to hastily add a chair or chairs in order to have a sit down dinner.

Never seat anyone at the corner edge of a square or rectangular table.
Never seat anyone directly facing a toilet door.
Never seat anyone directly facing the door into the dining room.
Never seat anyone directly underneath an overhead beam.
Never seat anyone directly facing a protruding corner.

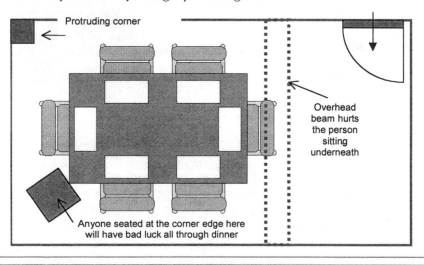

Protruding corner

Overhead
beam hurts
the person
sitting
underneath

Anyone seated at the corner edge here
will have bad luck all through dinner

CHAPTER
TWO

FENG SHUI
IN
ALL YOUR
RELATION
SHIPS

ENHANCING
FRIENDSHIPS

Seating yourself at poker or mahjong | TIP 51

When you are at a poker or mahjong game, the feng shui guidelines to follow are defensive in nature. You would want to sit in a way that ensures that even if you do not win, that you will at least not lose! Here again, you can make the fullest use of your auspicious directions.

Try as much as possible to sit facing your best direction. This means your *sheng chi* direction (see page 2). If you find it not possible to sit facing this best direction, then you should make very certain you do not sit facing one of your four inauspicious directions. If y0ou do, and especially if you sit facing your *chueh ming* direction, (which means total loss) it is highly likely that you will lose money!

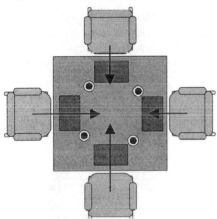

THE MAHJONG GAME

1. The arrows show you how you should take your directions to ensure luck in each of the four chairs.
2. Do not allow anyone to sit on your right. This brings bad luck. An observer on your left is acceptable.
3. Observe all the sitting taboos listed out on the previous page while sitting at the mahjong table.

ENHANCING LUCK AT THE POKER or MAHJONG TABLE

1. Sit facing one of your best directions.
2. Wear your good luck color. Use the year of birth to determine your year element and dress according to this element. Or use a compass to check the compass direction of where you are sitting and then dress according to the element of your corner.
3. Make certain that, from where you are seated, it is well lit. A bright light directly above you brings good luck as long as it is not glaring. Spotlights can be much too yang so they are best avoided.
4. Keep three coins tied with red thread in your purse, and also on the table directly in front of you. This attracts good luck to you. Place the coins amongst your chips to energize them.

CHAPTER
TWO

FENG SHUI IN
ALL YOUR
RELATION
SHIPS

ENHANCING
FRIENDSHIPS

Knives and Scissors in Friendships | TIP 52

When working at your desk, be careful never to leave scissors on the table with the pointed part facing you (or someone else). This transforms the harmless pair of scissors into a poison arrow inadvertently pointing directly at you and sending hostile energies towards you. This same advice holds true for penknives, screwdrivers and other tools like hammers drilling bits and so forth. Develop awareness for objects like these that lie around the home, and incorporate this awareness into your own personal habits.

When you point a sharp object that is also hostile – like a knife or a pair of scissors – at a friend, the effect will be the creation of an almost immediate friction between the two of you. Nothing kills friendships faster than the inadvertent presence of a sharp object driving a wedge between. Thus never give anything sharp as a present to anyone. Not even to your worse enemy since the results are usually unpleasant.

KNIVES make HORRIBLE GIFTS

A gift of anything that is sharp pointed or hostile carries some extremely hostile energy and causes bad feng shui for the recipient of your gift. As such Chinese people never buy tools, knives and other sharp objects to be given as gifts. If you are inadvertently given something sharp as a gift item (such as a tool box, a handy Swiss knife or a corkscrew opener for your wines) you can nullify the bad effects of the gift by immediately paying for the gift by giving a token dollar note to the person who has given you the gift. This symbolizes that you have "bought" the gift yourself thereby protecting yourself from the negative energy inherent in something hostile being given to you. I strongly recommend that this antidote be followed since the repercussions can sometimes be quite tragic. Do not dismiss this as superstition. Remember that superstitions are often the orally transmitted wisdom of our ancestors.

CHAPTER
TWO

FENG SHUI
IN
ALL YOUR
RELATION
SHIPS

ENHANCING
FRIENDSHIPS

Create good luck for those around you | TIP 53

There is no better way of making and keeping the friends and neighbours in your life than to design your feng shui in a way that not only does not hurt them, but instead, enhance their sense of well being. You should learn feng shui with the motivation of making certain that anything you build would not create bad feng shui for those who live around you.

By making certain you do not create bad feng shui for others, the energy that surrounds your environment will be filled with healthy *chi* that has not been defiled by the presence of negative poison arrows. These can very well get created and caused inadvertently by your roof line, your house façade and your corner edges. It is for this reason that I am always reluctant to recommend the use of Pa Kua Mirrors to solve simple feng shui problems. The Pa Kua mirror is a powerful tool, but it works by hurting others.

Thus when a poison arrow is threatening my front door I prefer to use a windchime, or to plant plants that block out the poison arrow rather than hang a Pa Kua which will definitely hurt my neighbor. If you keep this tip in mind, you will be adding to the creation of beautiful energy in your neighborhood thereby benefiting everyone who lives around you.

Place lights on your borders to create excellent energies of good fortune for your neighbors. Especially when placed in the vicinity of their front gate or front door, this act of good neighborliness brings harmony to your relationships with them. If there is a fence between you and your neighbours, make sure they do not have designs that could hurt your neighbors. Sharp pointed arrows or triangles aimed at your neighbor's home cause ill fortune to befall them. It will rebound on you when your neighbor retaliates with Pa Kua mirrors, or worst yet, cannons and other sharp pointed objects that point directly at your front door, There will be no end to a feng shui war!

Broken glass bits on walls

I have seen walls that are stuck with lots of broken glass bits that have obviously been placed there to keep intruders out. This also creates extreme bad energy. The presence of these sharp hostile objects will create bad feng shui for everyone who sees it including the house residents who installed them in the first place. I strongly recommend that if you have them, they should be removed. Feng shui methods of protection are much better.

CHAPTER
TWO

FENG SHUI
IN
ALL YOUR
RELATION
SHIPS

ENHANCING
FRIENDSHIPS

Pointing a finger creates bad feng shui | TIP 54

It is wise never to allow anyone to point the index finger at you when they speak to you. This directs bad energy towards you. If you are subjected to too much finger pointing, you will definitely succumb to a large dose of bad luck. Likewise you too should refrain from pointing at someone when you speak.

In certain cultures it is regarded as extremely rude and ill mannered to point a finger as you speak. It puts people off you and the energies created will be most hostile. Do not incorporate finger pointing into your advertisement campaigns or any promotional literature you may be designing since this creates extremely bad energy.

The most well known advertisement using a pointing finger was the American Advertisement calling for recruits into the US army. *"Uncle Sam wants you"* " the advertisement says and a grouchy faced man draped in the US flag points a finger directly at the reader. This advertisement appeared on posters everywhere during the Vietnam War.

It was not a good advertisement from a feng shui point of view.

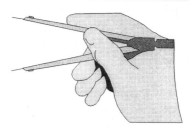

Here are variations of harmful hand gestures. It is a good idea to develop awareness and sensitivity to way you are spoken to, and to the way you speak to others. Energy exists in the environment and jabbing at people with pointed objects always creates hostile energies.

Never point a pair of scissors at anyone as you talk. It is bad !

CHAPTER
TWO

FENG SHUI
IN
ALL YOUR
RELATION
SHIPS

ENHANCING
FRIENDSHIPS

Heaven men and Devil men | TIP 55

In the language of feng shui, descriptions of <u>helpful</u> and <u>unhelpful</u> people are usually so colourful it is impossible not to be amused. However, when you receive help unexpectedly from an influential person, or when your career gets a huge boost due to the positive recommendation of someone important in your work, then you begin to understand why feng shui describe such people as *heaven men*.

Likewise, when you are the victim of a powerful person's vindictiveness, or when someone you trust, betrays you, causing you to lose money. lose a promotion or a project you had been angling for, you will begin to understand why feng shui describes such people in your life as *devil men*.

According to feng shui, certain features in your feng shui can affect the presence or absence of helpful and unhelpful people in your life. This is mainly impacted by the quality of the CHIEN corner of your home(or office). The CHIEN corner of your home is the Norwest since this is the corner that is ruled by the trigram CHIEN. This is the ultimate yang trigram, and its corner in any home is vitally important and must be safeguarded at all times irrespective what your personal auspicious and inauspicious directions are !

YOUR CHIEN CORNER

This is the NORTHWEST corner of your home according to the compass. This corner is NOT determined by the placement of the front door. It is determined by an ordinary boy scout compass !

Hang a metal windchime with 8 hollow rods in your *Chien* corner to attract heaven men into your life. By doing this you will also be energizing the luck of the Patriarch. It is thus doubly rewarding. You can also use metal bells to implement this tip.

"Devil men" come in the form of obnoxious bosses, troublesome colleagues and insincere friends. Learn to recognize the presence of such people in your life.

"Heaven men" usually take the form of helpful Mentors who give you a guiding hand, protect you and create wonderful opportunities for you. Use feng shui to energize the luck of attracting Mentors luck into your life.

Watch out for bright lights in the Northwest since this will attract devil men into your life. The presence of fire element in the Northwest is extremely harmful. Make sure you do not place spotlights or chandeliers in this corner of your home or living room.

CHAPTER
TWO

FENG SHUI
IN
ALL YOUR
RELATION
SHIPS

ENHANCING
FRIENDSHIPS

One for the road – the last drink...

TIP 56

A popular way to end a dinner evening or a party is for the host to offer *One for the Road*, the offer of a last drink before the guests depart.
When you are offered a last drink, feng shui advises that you should <u>Not</u> refuse. Even if you take only a symbolic sip of water, this will make certain that you get home safely.

According to Chinese feng shui beliefs, the guest should never refuse the offer of the last drink, the last helping - the *"just one more piece of cake before you leave dear"*.

To refuse generates the bad luck of travel. You could meet up with obstacles getting home. Thus when you are a guest, make certain you always take a small symbolic bite on a piece of biscuit if offered, before you take your leave.

<u>Does taking the last piece make one a perennial bachelor or an unmarried old maid ?</u>

Will it create obstacles for singles in search of a mate?

This is an old superstition that was passed to me when I was in my teens. I was told that if I ate the last piece of chicken on the plate, accepted the last portion of cake or generally always take the left over morsel at the end of a meal – I would have a hard time landing a husband. All through my teenage years I strenuously avoided taking the last piece of food at any meal. I did not discover the authenticity of this particular superstition until I told an old feng shui practitioner in Hong Kong who confirmed it. He told me that regularly taking the last morsel also created <u>poverty</u> energies and caused descendants luck to become afflicted.

The last piece of food – to take it or not ?

CHAPTER
TWO

FENG SHUI
IN
ALL YOUR
RELATION
SHIPS

ENHANCING
FRIENDSHIPS

Feng shui for serving refreshments

TIP 57

When serving tea, coffee or drinks to your visitors make sure you do not point the spout of the tea pot or coffee pot directly at anyone. These spouts are like tiny poison arrows aimed at them.

When you are a guest, it is a good idea to lean over and move the tea pot or jug, if the spout happens to be pointing directly·at you. Otherwise the spout is sending little slivers of killing breath towards you. When entertaining therefore, please be conscious of this little point. Otherwise the poison arrows create small discords that can magnify into misunderstandings. I was told that in China of the old days, Triads often used the spout of the teapot as a secret signal between members to pinpoint adversaries to fellow members. Thus if there is an outsider at the table unknown to other members, someone will lean over to reposition the tea pot so that the spout points directly at the "outsider" thereby sending secret poison arrows his way.

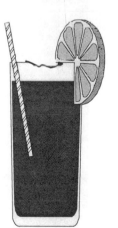

Another piece of advice when entertaining friends is never to serve coffee or tea in a cup with a chipped mouth. Or serve drinks with a chipped glass. Drinking from a tea cup or coffee cup which has even the smallest chip brings bad luck since this symbolically cuts the mouth thereby negatively affecting one's speech.

Crockery in the home should never be chipped or broken. It is a good idea to go through your crockery at home and to discard pieces of flawed porcelain. This makes sure you never use them. Either for yourself of for your guests.

The Chinese believe that drinking from chipped cups and glasses or eating from chipped bowls seriously affects one's "rice bowl", which is another way of saying it causes one to suffer from bad luck in one's livelihood. If you are in business this rule becomes even more important since it affects your business. Be especially mindful with tea cups.

CHAPTER
THREE

FENG SHUI
IN THE
OFFICE

ENHANCING
YOUR
WORK
SPACE

Choosing your personal work space   TIP 58

If you want to enjoy good feng shui at work, you should try to select your 'work space" carefully. Naturally some people will have a greater say in where they may have their office than others. Nevertheless you should do what you can to observe the following feng shui guidelines on choosing your personal workspace.

This is the best spot in the whole office.

- Always try to have your office and desk in the far corner diagonal to the entrance door into the whole office. The deeper you are inside the office the better will be the feng shui.

- Never have your office or desk located at the end of a straight corridor or walkway.

- Do not sit in an office or desk that directly faces the entrance door.

- Do not sit in an office or desk that directly faces a toilet door or a staircase. Your chances for advancement will be severely curtailed.

- Do not sit in an office or a desk that places you directly underneath an exposed overhead beam. You will suffer from endless pressure and headaches.

- Do not sit with your back to the door, whether it is the door into your private office, or the door into the office itself.

- Never sit in a desk or place which subjects you to being hit by the cutting edge of a protruding corner. Move out of the line of fire and use a plant to block.

- Try to avoid sitting directly opposite a square pillar. The cutting edge of the pillar will create havoc in your work life. Success will be hard to come by, and you will get ill frequently. The best solution is to move out, but if you cannot, then you should try to deflect the bad energy with plants, or with mirrors that are wrapped around the entire four sides of the pillar. This serves symbolically, to make the column or pillar *disappear..*

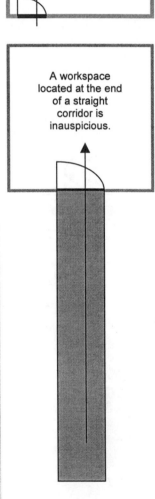

A workspace located at the end of a straight corridor is inauspicious.

CHAPTER
THREE

FENG SHUI
IN THE
OFFICE

ENHANCING
YOUR
WORK
SPACE

Energizing your compass group | TIP 59

Go to page 2 and check out your four auspicious directions. From the directions determine if you are an East group or a West group person.

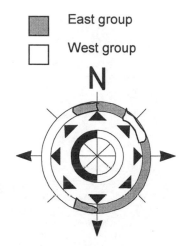

■ East group

☐ West group

The EAST GROUP DIRECTIONS
Are EAST, NORTH,
SOUTH and SOUTHEAST

WEST GROUP DIRECTIONS
Are WEST, SOUTHWEST,
NORTHWEST AND NORTHEAST

EAST GROUP ENERGIZERS:

- Energize the East corner with plants, flowers and paintings that have lush vegetation and water. Avoid at all costs, anything metallic in this corner. windchimes, scissors and blades cause a lot of harm.
- The same for the Southeast except here you can also display a miniature fountain, or a simple bowl of water.
- In the North place a broad based bowl of water with a terrapin inside. This can be real or fake. The real one is to be preferred.
- In the South place something red – a painting, a red carpet, red cushions and place a bright light to energize the luck of a great reputation. Properly energized the South brings excellent reputation luck.

WEST GROUP ENERGIZERS

- Energize the west with a model airplane laden with coins tied with red thread. Bells and windchimes are also effective.
- Energize the Northwest the same way. Do not put bright lights in either the west or the northwest as these will magnify all your problems.
- Energize the Southwest with lots of natural crystals. If your main door is also located in.the Southwest, then placing a large real crystal stone is most effective. A good friend of mine placed a large amethyst crystal boulder that had a deep "pocket" to capture all the good fortune coming into the office. It brought him masses of business luck !
- Energize the Northeast the same way as the Southwest but it is not necessary to display crystals that are too large.

CHAPTER
THREE

FENG SHUI
IN THE
OFFICE

ENHANCING
YOUR
WORK
SPACE

Activating your lucky directions

TIP 60

The best place to use the auspicious directions of one's KUA number is in the office. Check page 2 again to refresh yourself on your lucky directions and then do at least one of two things.

- Sit directly facing your *sheng chi* i.e. Your most auspicious direction while working.
- Place your office in the location that corresponds to your *sheng chi*.

The correct application of the KUA formula directions in feng shui can be extremely potent. This is not to be confused with the nine star *Ki* formula used by some feng shui practitioners.

The KUA formula is based on the two major symbols of feng shui practice – the *Pa Kua* and its eight trigrams arranged around the sides according to the Later heaven arrangement and the nine sector *Lo Shu* square.

To simplify the formula for readers I have summarized the lucky and unlucky directions according to an individual's personal KUA number. But knowing one's auspicious directions is only half of the practice. To get the most out of this feng shui formula, the directions must be skillfully applied.

It may not always be possible to sit in one's most favourable location, or face one's most auspicious direction, due perhaps to the presence of poison arrows. If this is the situation, then it becomes a matter of great urgency that you try to be located in, and to sit facing at least one of – your three other auspicious directions. This is to ensure you do not succumb to the negative forces of your four unlucky directions.

Meanwhile, of the four, the first direction is the best for career and business but it is the fourth direction that is the best for self development.

CHAPTER
THREE

FENG SHUI
IN THE
OFFICE

ENHANCING
YOUR
WORK
SPACE

Protecting against bad feng shui

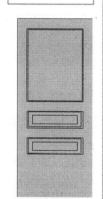

Bad feng shui in most offices is frequently traced to the entrance door being afflicted. Or hurt by outside features.

- If the door that opens into your office is at the end of a corridor, it receives killing chi everyday.
- If the office door faces a bank of elevators, the constant opening and closing of the elevator doors creates a great deal of imbalance.
- If the door faces a staircase, the chi is extremely negative, and if there are two staircases, one going up and the other going down, then there will be a great deal of disharmony and quarrels in the office.

FEATURES THAT CAN CAUSE BAD FENG SHUI IN THE OFFICE

OPEN
Bookshelves
resemble
blades that
send out
killing energy

**THE SHARP EDGE
OF A TABLE**

**A TABLE PILED HIGH WITH
FILES. EXCESSIVE JUMBLE
CREATES TOO MUCH YIN.**

A WORD about clutter
I have always maintained that keeping one's home and office clean is as much common sense as it is feng shui. Excessive disarray in the office however, does cause confusion thereby creating disharmony. Do not allow your office to get so untidy that you drown in a sea of paperwork!

CHAPTER
THREE

FENG SHUI
IN THE
OFFICE

ENHANCING
YOUR
WORK
SPACE

Avoiding killing chi

TIP 62

In the office you should always be on the lookout for anything that is sharp, pointed, heavy and threatening looking. Many of these secret poison arrows within your personal space are easily overlooked, unless you take the trouble to consciously look out for them.

The killing breath of the dragon inside any office is usually less lethal than the killing breath caused by massive structures of the landscape environment. Nevertheless, sharp edges of furniture, cupboards, filing cabinets and the like often cause severe headaches, and occupants succumb to tiredness and listlessness at best, and severe illnesses at worst.

Probably the most effective and aesthetic way of combating secret pointed arrows inside an office is to display large vases of flowers as shown above. Having said that it is also important not to overdo things and turn your office into a flower shop!

For example, when there are many square pillars inside an office – and this is usually the case in dealing rooms and newspaper offices, which have open plan arrangements – a solution must be found. In this situation you can very effectively break up the *killing chi* by arranging fake silk trees that serve to soften the edges of pillars. Bringing fake trees into the office has another feng shui benefit in those trees symbolized growth that is excellent for business. Of the five elements, wood, as symbolized by trees and plants is the best element to activate within the office. Fake trees are acceptable for feng shui purposes but they should be kept free of dust, and they should be regularly cleaned. They should not look sick and droopy.
Offices that use real plants should make sure to throw them out as soon they turn yellow or shed their leaves. There is nothing worse than dying plants in an office or a house. They emanate massive amounts of negative poisonous killing chi.

CHAPTER
THREE

FENG SHUI
IN THE
OFFICE

ENHANCING
YOUR
WORK
SPACE

Softening the sharp edges of your space | TIP 63

When doing your feng shui, always remember that anything sharp is harmful. It needs to be softened, blocked or put out of sight. Anything sharp causes feng shui problems.

Anything curved and softly flowing encourages the energy in the environment to slow down, settle and get transformed into friendly energy.

Look at the shapes and lines drawn on this page. It is not difficult to train the eye to differentiate between what is potentially good and what is potentially bad feng shui. Thus art décor would tend to create harmful feng shui while art nouveau would create auspicious feng shui.

Anything that is straight will cause problems while anything circular brings good fortune.

If you but master these two simple rules of form school feng shui you will be going a long way to train your feng shui "eye". When in doubt always select the option that allows the invisible energy lines in your personal space to slow down. Thus using plants, screens, curtains, and other soft furnishings allow you to achieve this result. When shapes are angular and threatening, either soften the edges or if that is impossible, hang fabrics, use potted plants and when all else fails shine a bright light to counter the excessive sharp energy.

When selecting your particular feng shui 'cure' or balancing agent, be guided by the rules that govern the production and destruction of the five elements. When you practice feng shui this way, you are going to the core of the practice and you will begin to realize how easy it is. You will be able to undertake feng shui diagnosis yourself.

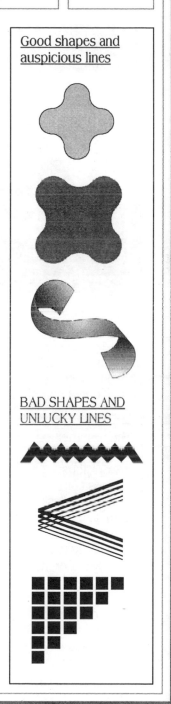

Good shapes and auspicious lines

BAD SHAPES AND UNLUCKY LINES

CHAPTER
THREE

FENG SHUI
IN THE
OFFICE

ENHANCING
YOUR
WORK
SPACE

Feng shui Tips on sitting problems

TIP 64

Develop the habit of looking around your personal space.
Look up above you to check whether you are sitting under an exposed overhead beam. These heavy overhead structures are very bad news and you really want to avoid them at all costs.
Big exposed beams cause severe headaches, migraine, stress and a great deal of bad luck.

Look sideways to see if there are any pointed edges of walls, furniture and protruding corners that may be sending poison arrows your way. Edges cut into you causing illness, stress, pressure and again, a great deal of bad luck. At work these pointed edges create havoc with your career prospects. You cannot operate at efficient capacities so you should deal with such structures immediately, as soon as you become aware of them.

The best method of correcting these inauspicious features is to move your desk from under the beam, or away from being directly under the sharp edge.

If you cannot do this then try the cures suggested on the right here.

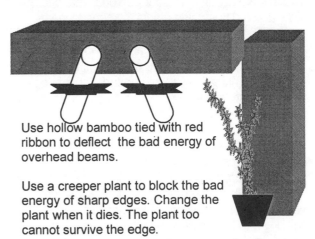

Use hollow bamboo tied with red ribbon to deflect the bad energy of overhead beams.

Use a creeper plant to block the bad energy of sharp edges. Change the plant when it dies. The plant too cannot survive the edge.

CHAPTER
THREE

FENG SHUI
IN THE
OFFICE

ENHANCING
YOUR
WORK
SPACE

Take note of seating arrangements | TIP 65

You should be careful not to sit facing the corner of a square table. If the sharp edge is pointed directly at you, harmful energy aimed straight at you will harm you. If you are eating, you will not have a good meal. If you are playing a card game you will lose and if you are with someone you care for, a misunderstanding will arise.

When there are five people seated in a small square table meant only for four people, make sure you do not take the chair that is placed directly facing the edge of the table. The "*poison arrow*" of the edge shoots out hostile energy that will cause you to be unlucky for the rest of the day.

This man here is being hurt by his seating position

At work, each time there is a meeting, consciously make sure you do not find yourself seated with a pointed edge directly piercing into your tummy! This seating arrangement will place you at a disadvantage to the rest of your colleagues.
At a Board meeting, or when there is an important negotiation taking place, make certain you observe this feng shui guideline strenuously.

When attending an important interview, for a scholarship or a job; or when meeting your supervisor or your boss, you must endeavour never to sit facing the edge of the table, as shown above. If you do, luck will be against you., and It will be very unlikely for you to be successful or to get what you want. Always sit facing one of your four good directions.

CHAPTER
THREE

FENG SHUI
IN THE
OFFICE

ENHANCING
YOUR
WORK
SPACE

Orientating your negotiating position

TIP 66

In the situation depicted above, the man who will have the feng shui advantage is the one who is sitting directly facing his best i.e. *Sheng chi* direction.

You can use feng shui to enhance your negotiating luck. Do this by simply sitting and facing one of your four auspicious directions. If the person you are negotiating with is sitting in his or her bad direction you will definitely have the edge.

This holds true in any kind of interview or business negotiations. Get your auspicious directions from the table on page 2.

If you cannot remember your auspicious directions, or you do not have a compass, do not attempt to guess at your good direction. This will put you off course. Instead, use Form School feng shui instead and apply the following guidelines.

- Choose the seat that is furthest away from the door into the room.
- Never sit with your back to the door. In any negotiating scenario you MUST be able to '*see*' the door. Otherwise you could get stabbed from behind, and also when you least expect it.
- Try not to sit with your back to the window, unless it faces a solid building. If you sit with your back to the window you are deemed to be sorely lacking in support.
- Avoid sitting directly underneath beams and ceiling designs that are sharp and heavy. Move your chair and swivel it around if necessary.
- Choose a chair that has an armrest and a high back. This provides the traditional feng shui support that allows you to have balance.
- Do not sit in a seat that forces you to have your feet pointed at the door. This is a very inauspicious orientation.
- Finally never sit with anything sharp or angular pointing directly at you. Move your chair away to avoid being in the line of fire !

CHAPTER
THREE

FENG SHUI
IN THE
OFFICE

ENHANCING
YOUR
WORK
SPACE

Directions for important meetings

TIP 67

During my heady corporate days, I used my auspicious directions almost all the time, especially when I knew I was attending an important meeting. I always had a compass in my pocket and I always made certain that at meetings I took charge of the seating arrangements.

Usually, in addition to observing form school feng shui rules (most of which already been covered in this chapter), I always chose a seat that allowed me to face a direction that brought me luck. This meant always sitting facing one of my four good directions.

Always keep a compass in your briefcase!

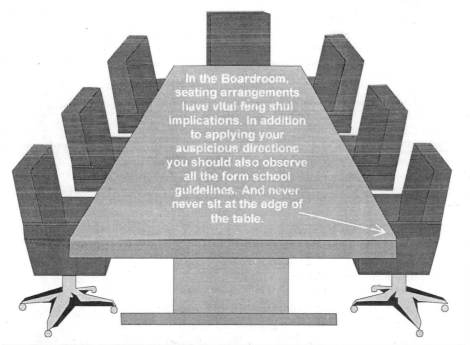

In the Boardroom, seating arrangements have vital feng shui implications. In addition to applying your auspicious directions you should also observe all the form school guidelines. And never never sit at the edge of the table.

Feng shui can be usefully applied in almost any part of your corporate or business life. Each time you have a sales meeting, a budget meeting, a board meeting, or an interview remember to sue your directions!

CHAPTER
THREE

FENG SHUI
IN THE
OFFICE

YOUR OWN
OFFICE
ARRANGE
MENTS

ENERGIZING YOUR DESK TOP

TIP 68

- You must be seated facing your *sheng chi*.
- Leave the part of the desk directly in front of you empty of files, books etc. Create a mini "bright hall"

North

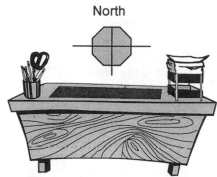

First get the directions of the corners of your desk top by using a good compass

- Piles of files should be higher on the left than on the right.
- Place the telephone in the corner that matches an auspicious personal direction

Flowers

Place a vase of fresh flowers on the East side of your desk top. Do not allow flowers to overwhelm or block your view. Change the flowers as soon as the leaves turn yellow. Flowers create yang energy.

Plants

Place a very healthy small plant on the Southeast corner of your desk top. This attracts good income and enhances your chances of personal growth.

Crystal Paperweight

Place a round crystal on the Southwest corner of your desk top to create the luck of harmonious relationships with your colleagues.

Lamp

Any kind of light energizes your good name and reputation when placed in the South. This is one of the most excellent methods of creating a solid reputation within your company, and your business community.

Calculators and Computers ...

All personal office equipment made of metal should be placed on a separate table that is preferably located on the West or Northwest of your desk . If you need to have them on your desk top, place them on your right hand side, BUT make certain you also have something higher to place on the left side. This ensures that the energies of the *dragon* prevail over the *tiger*

CHAPTER
THREE

FENG SHUI
IN THE
OFFICE

YOUR OWN
OFFICE
ARRANGE
MENTS

Enhance and Protect your career | TIP 69

Feng shui is extremely potent when it comes to creating career luck. Indeed, during the old days when emperors reigned over China, the mandarins at court were especially mindful of ensuring good fortune. In those days of autocratic imperial rule, bad luck could well create the kind of misfortune that led to death, not merely for the official but usually also for the entire family. Career survival was thus a very serious matter. Feng shui was often applied to ensure that there was always protection from being the victim of court intrigues.

In today's modern commercial and corporate environment, we have the equivalent of court intrigues, and difficulties of this nature are broadly referred to as company politics.

Feng shui can provide an excellent shield against being overwhelmed by internal politicking. Feng shui can safeguard you from being elbowed put of opportunities for advancement. And feng shui can help reduce the chances of you getting stabbed in the back by people who are jealous of your position or advancements. Thus you can both enhance and have protection in your career with feng shui.

ENHANCE your CAREER
by energizing the North corner of your office. This is the universal corner associated with one's fortunes at work. The ruling trigram of the North is the trigram KAN which means water. It feng shui, water is respected as the bringer of great good fortune. But water is also regarded as extremely dangerous when it breaks its banks. Thus you can tap the element of water for the North to create career luck but you must not overdo it. Too much water will drown you!

Place a small water feature, preferably with the water continuously moving to signify movement and yang energy. A miniature water fountain about one feet diameter would be ideal !

PROTECT your CAREER
By observing some simple feng shui guidelines. In the office NEVER sit with your back to the door, never sit with the door behind you. Doing so invites deception and betrayal. You could well become the victim of treachery and dishonesty.

To provide additional protection sit with the painting of a mountain behind you. The mountain gives you support. NEVER sit with the painting of a mountain in front of you ! This represents you confronting the mountain, and in such an encounter you are certain to be overcome. Let the mountain protect you instead.

CHAPTER
THREE

FENG SHUI
IN THE
OFFICE

YOUR OWN
OFFICE
ARRANGE
MENTS

Creating support with the mountain

Always sit with back support. If your office is located on the top floor of a multi storey building and you sit with your back to a window, chances are you will lack solid support in your work and career.

If there is a view of mountain, then sit with your back protected by this mountain. Do not sit facing the mountain even if that happens to be your most auspicious *sheng chi* direction. In feng shui a form as large as a mountain almost always takes precedence over compass school formulas.

In feng shui the energies of Mountains and rivers, when skillfully captured. Is extremely potent.

When choosing a picture of a mountain, make sure it is big enough to be meaningful. A mountain range of hills like the above is good but not excellent. Do not have mountain ranges that are too sharp since these fire element mountains are less useful. The best type of mountain for protection is the turtle shaped mountain i.e. A mountain that resembles the back of a turtle, like the one shown below.

A river coming towards you like this is dangerous !

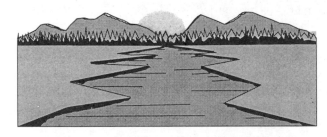

Do not hang a picture of a mountain that has a river, a lake, or any kind of water feature behind you. Water behind you is a sign of missed luck.

CHAPTER
THREE

FENG SHUI
IN THE
OFFICE

YOUR OWN
OFFICE
ARRANGE
MENTS

A turtle for stunning success

TIP 71

If you prefer, you can substitute the picture of a mountain with that of the turtle. In feng shui folk lore the turtle is regarded as a most auspicious and celestial creature which brings extreme good fortune. Everyone benefits from the symbolic presence of the turtle which is also a symbol of longevity. It is also the guardian of the North, which governs career luck !

Keeping a live terrapin

If you have a large enough office, one of the best feng shui tips I can pass on to you is to keep a single terrapin or tortoise in the <u>NORTH</u> wall or corner of your office. It is not necessary to keep more than one tortoise. The number of the North is one, and a single terrapin or tortoise is more auspicious than a pair. This is an exception to the guideline for relationships enhancement where keeping mandarin ducks in a pair is considered more auspicious. In the case of the tortoise, what we are trying to do is to activate the element as well as the celestial creature of the North to bring about excellent career luck. This tip is applicable even if the North direction is one of your bad directions under the KUA formula. The symbolism of the tortoise transcends all formula schools of feng shui.

The tortoise is a reptile that likes both water and dry land. You can use an aquarium to keep your tortoise, or you can be as creative as you wish. Place a boulder in the container, and fill it half full with water. Feed your tortoise fresh watercress or " *kangkong*" . They love green vegetables. But you can also feed them with terrapin food bought from a pet shop. There is no need to over feed since they survive on very little. But is important to change the water regularly. Remember to let the water stand for a little while to get rid of the chlorine in the water. Standing a pail of water in the sun for at least three hours before using it for the tortoise gives it *yang* energized water.

CHAPTER
THREE

FENG SHUI
IN THE
OFFICE

YOUR OWN
OFFICE
ARRANGE
MENTS

Create a water symbol in front of you | TIP 72

A view of water without mountains is better than a view of water with mountains. If the mountain is far away like what is shown here the picture is acceptable. If the mountain is too near in the picture, it can represent obstacles in your work inspite of the water.

If you can find a beautiful painting of water to hang in front of you in the office, and if the wall facing you is either North, East or Southeast, it will bring exceptionally good fortune into your work life.

If the wall that faces you is <u>not</u> one of these directions, this tip is not for you. Remember that water is a double-edged tool. It can be very potent, but only when used correctly. If you do not have the premises that allow tapping the good energies of water, then my advice is that you pass, on this particular tip.

If you use a water symbol, like the wave symbols shown on the left here, make them small so they do not seem to overwhelm you.

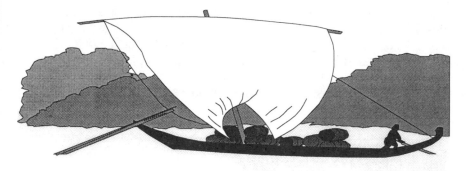

A picture or painting of a sailing boat, loaded with wealth and sailing towards you is the most excellent symbol. The picture above shows the wind direction clearly. The boat is sailing towards you.
The boat is also filled with products that spell money.
This is a good fortune picture.

CHAPTER
THREE

FENG SHUI
IN THE
OFFICE

YOUR OWN
OFFICE
ARRANGE
MENTS

Position your telephone for luck | TIP 73

Note the
source of the
telephone's energy

Note source of the fax machine's energy

If you want to *feng shui* the telephone and fax machine in your office, you must first observe from what direction the energy that brings the messages through the phone and fax is coming from. This is considered the source of the telephone's energy.

The next thing to do is to position the phone so that the *source* of messages, calls and so forth are coming from your most auspicious direction. This is your *sheng chi* direction. The application of this feng shui method is a modern application of an ancient formula which advises that energy that comes to you should come from your most favourable direction. This is considered to be equally applicable in all aspects of your working and family life. It is important however, to remember that it is the source of energy that is important so make sure you get this right.

Example:

- If your *sheng chi* is East then you should place your phone in such a way that the incoming wire enters the phone from the East.
- If your *sheng chi* direction is impossible to tap you should try to get one of the other three auspicious directions i.e. North, South, or Southeast.

The source of the energy coming into this fax machine is the direction of the arrow

Do not make the mistake of thinking it is the electricity AC plug we are talking about. Your fax will bring you good news and opportunities only if the **source** of the news is from your good direction

CHAPTER
THREE

FENG SHUI
IN THE
OFFICE

YOUR OWN
OFFICE
ARRANGE
MENTS

Place a crimson bird in your South   TIP 74

The South is the abode of the crimson phoenix which symbolizes strength in adversity. The phoenix also brings the luck of opportunities. When you energize this king of all feathered creatures, you are also activating the beneficial energies of the South. The luck of this particular sector suggests a great brightness because the South is also the place of the element of fire.

Thus a crimson feathered creature to symbolize the phoenix would be extremely auspicious.

A picture of an eagle in full flight is an excellent symbol of success. In addition to representing the winged creature of the South, the eagle is also associated with strength, power and authority. Show an eagle flying or perched on a tree. Do not show an eagle looking fierce and predatory.

Since it is really quite difficult to find a suitable picture or sculpture of the legendary phoenix, you can use any kind of beautiful bird that has colourful (and preferably red) plumage to represent the beneficial presence of the phoenix. The swan, the rooster, the peacock, and even the longevity birds – the crane and the flamingo are all suitable.

There are stunning bird sculptures made of ceramics and crystal that you can purchase and display in the South corner – either on a table or inside a cabinet. The effect is most auspicious. Not only will your reputation get enhanced over the years, but you will achieve recognition and attain great success in your profession.

If you can get an art piece of the crimson phoenix itself that would be even better. During my days at the helm of my department store in Hong Kong, I displayed a stunning gold embedded crystal phoenix in the South corner of my office to reflect my goal of giving my department store a successful new image. The feng shui of the phoenix worked beautifully!

CHAPTER
THREE

FENG SHUI
IN THE
OFFICE

YOUR OWN
OFFICE
ARRANGE
MENTS

The number 8 and other lucky numbers | TIP 75

Numbers have feng shui implications on career and business success. There are individual lucky and unlucky numbers, and Chinese businessmen are most particular about the numbers of their telephones, their addresses, their car numbers and their bank accounts. They will never allow the critical numbers of their commercial life to have what they deem unlucky numbers.

LUCKY NUMBERS
In addition to the number 8, other lucky numbers are 1, 6 and 9. Prefixed with a 4 these numbers become even luckier. The number 9 is especially superior since 9 added to itself to infinity still becomes 9. Thus 9 multiplied by any number of times, and then reduced to a single number always becomes 9 again. Nine represents the fullness of heaven and earth. The other lucky number is 7 because this is the period of 7

The number 8 is widely regarded by Chinese as a universally lucky number. The feng shui explanation given is that phonetically it sounds like *"growth with prosperity"* Much of feng shui symbolism is based on the sound of the symbol used. There are tycoons in Hong Kong who happily part with a cool million dollars for the privilege of having the single number 8 on their car number plates.

The number 13 is not considered an unlucky number. The number 14 is

UNLUCKY NUMBERS
The most unlucky number according to the Chinese is the number 4 because it sounds like 'death" in many dialects. Thus any series of numbers that end with a 4 is a major taboo. The unlucky numbers based on *flying star feng shui* are the numbers 5 and 2 and also the numbers 2 and 3 together. Some people regard 2 as a good number that means *easy.*

On telephone numbers, credit cards and bank accounts, the Chinese also like to end their series of numbers with the letter 8 as they believe that this brings good fortune to their financial accounts. When the number is prefixed with 6,7,8 or 9 the luck is regarded to have doubled

CHAPTER
THREE

FENG SHUI
IN THE
OFFICE

YOUR OWN
OFFICE
ARRANGE
MENTS

Block out excessive sunlight

TIP 76

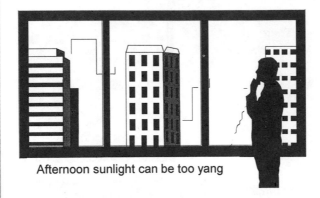

Afternoon sunlight can be too yang

Block with Curtains

Use fairly heavy drape curtains to block out the afternoon sun completely. If you live in the Tropics like I do, the afternoon sun can be so glaring and hot – it completely dissipates my energy. The most effective of combating this excessive yang energy of the sun is to use the water element. Thus curtains should be blue to simulate the water element. White curtains are also very effective since the West is the place of metal and white is symbolic of metal. Although fire burns metal, and thus can overcome white, if you use thick drapes the sunlight will be kept out. You will find after doing this that the yang energy comes under control and people will be less quarrelsome.

Dissipate by hanging cut crystals

Another method of controlling excessive sunlight is to hang balls of Swarovski cut crystal to catch the sunlight. This creates wonderful rainbows inside the office by breaking up the light into colors.

This method seeks to harness the good energies of the sun and is best used in countries where the sun is not too hot. In the Tropics, unless the sunlight is kept out with curtains, drapes and shutters, the glare will turn the energy hostile despite the presence of the crystals and the rainbow sunlight.

While it is excellent to energize your desk top and the corners of your office, it is also important not to forget about the balance of yin and yang energies in the office. Generally speaking, the presence of precious yang energy is very important and beneficial in an office environment.

However when there is too much yang energy, the effect can be catastrophic. Excessive yang energy often comes in the form of strong sunlight caused by an office that has a west-facing wall. The brightness and heat of the afternoon sun, especially during the summer months can create an excess of fire energy. Such a situation will create disharmony in the office. Flared tempers and impatience will be the order of the day. You must do something about it if this describes your office situation.

CHAPTER
THREE

FENG SHUI
IN THE
OFFICE

YOUR OWN
OFFICE
ARRANGE
MENTS

Black, white and colors in feng shui | TIP 77

In feng shui, <u>black</u> represents water and <u>white</u> represents gold or metal. Although neither color is preferred over the other, it is important to note that generally black should never be used for the ceilings and the roofs. Surprising as it may seem I have seen black ceilings that instantly reminded me of a overhanging cloud. The feng shui was bad, and the furniture shop that sported it closed after 6 months. Black above, on the ceiling or roof always spells danger. Thus in your office I would strongly recommend that you avoid large patches of black. Don't use black on the walls, ceilings and carpets.

On the walls and ceilings use white instead. Apart from being a very yang color (as opposed to black being very yin) white's symbolism is prosperity. White is also considered a mourning color but it is not the bright pure white. The mourning white is like sack cloth and is regarded as off white – a yin color. The bright white I refer to is a yang color and comes highly recommended.

This black and white endless knot is an auspicious symbol. Use it as pattern or motif in your office décor, or frame it in your office for good luck.

RED

Is the color of the SOUTH, and shades of this color on your south wall could well bring you good fortune. I recommend that if you want to energize the red family of colors, go for a warm peachy shade of red and use it in the south, but also in the west to symbolically "*tame the tiger of the west*" You can apply feng shui color therapy in your wallpaper, your curtains and your carpets – in fact all your soft furnishings.

GREEN

Is the color of money especially when activated and given prominence in the Southeast. It is also very applicable for the East. Combine various shades of green if you wish but always remember that a bright green that symbolizes the growth of Spring is what you want to energize. Use fake silk trees with bright happy green leaves to energize better income luck for your office.

BLUE

Is the color of water. Use it to good effect in the East, the Southeast and North corners of your office space. Never overdo on the blue since water should never be activated in large quantities. It is also a good idea to mix blue with green.

CHAPTER
THREE

FENG SHUI
IN THE
OFFICE

YOUR OWN
OFFICE
ARRANGE
MENTS

Feng shui dimensions for chairs & tables | TIP 78

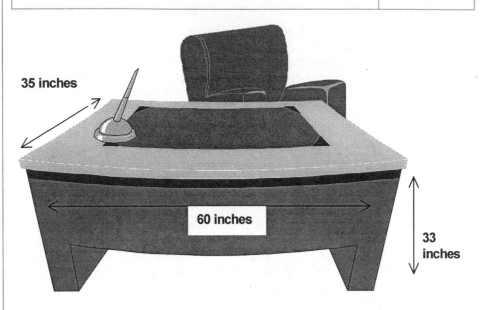

35 inches

60 inches

33 inches

The year I ordered a new desk made to feng shui dimensions, I was promoted so many times it became embarrassing. That was 1982, the year my career took a quantum leap. It was the year I was appointed the first woman CEO of a publicly listed company in Malaysia. It was also the year I became the first woman in Asia to head a bank. I was offered the job of Managing Director of the Grindlays Dao Heng Bank – then the sixth largest local bank in Hong Kong. Today the desk I use to write my best sellers have these exact same dimensions. I share this secret with you and wish you loads of luck.

Height: 33inches   Width: 35 inches   Length: 60 inches

The executive chair you sit on should have a high back to symbolize back support. Chairs that do not completely cover your back represent poor feng shui. The chair shown on the left can thus be improved if the back were a little higher.

Your chair should also have arm rests (as shown here). Chairs without armrests have the dragon and tiger missing. Once again that spells bad feng shui. Use a height of 43 inches for the back of your chair. This brings prosperity luck.

CHAPTER
THREE

FENG SHUI
IN THE
OFFICE

LUCKY AND
UNLIKELY
OBJECTS

Networking luck from the Northwest | TIP 79

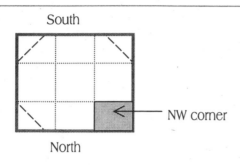

South

North

NW corner

A wealth bucket filled with coins is a wonderful way of reflecting and magnifying the metallic energies of the Northwest. Look for a decorative container that is made of metal and after filling it with coins, place it inside any cupboard or cabinet in the Northwest. Do not display this openly.

In decorative feng shui, my tip is to focus primarily on safeguarding and energizing the Northwest. Use a compass to determine the NW corner in your office. If you superimpose the
Lo Shu or Pa Kua over your office layout plan as shown above you can determine the NW corner as soon as you get your bearings.

The Northwest corners of your workspace and office have the greatest impact on your *helpful people and networking luck*. When the Northwest is correctly energized and yin yang balance is scrupulously maintained, you will find all your plans and ambitions succeed really easily. You will find that most people you do business with, or with whom you have to interact with, are always prepared to help you.

Decorative feng shui is based on an understanding of the concept of *wu xing* or five elements, and in this connection, the Northwest is the place of big metal. Thus this is the corner where all the gold and symbolic wealth of the office should be kept. The safe can definitely be kept here. In your own personal office, place your most important piece of metallic furniture here – it can be your safe, or your computer or even your photocopying machine.

GOLD

Place a bogus gold ingot in the Northwest to simulate the essence of gold. The Chinese display lots of this fake gold during the lunar New Year in the hope that the symbolic placement will stimulate the real thing. Decorative Feng shui is very symbolic, and it is for this reason that during the New Year, an incredible number of auspicious symbolic objects are used to decorate the home.

CHAPTER
THREE

FENG SHUI
IN THE
OFFICE

LUCKY AND
UNLIKELY
OBJECTS

Plants in the Southeast for profits luck

TIP 80

For as long as I have worked, I have always placed a foliage bushy plant in my office, During my pre feng shui knowledge days, I displayed plants because I always felt better when I had a plant inside my room. Today I do it because I have experienced the powerful effect which plants have on one's feng shui.

It is especially potent when placed in the Southeast corner of the office. Irrespective of whether you are a West or an East group person, everyone can activate the wonderful wealth energies of the Southeast. This is the corner characterized by small wood, which is in effect more valuable than big wood. Small wood are best symbolized by plants and by the color green.

SELECTION OF PLANTS
Fake plants are completely acceptable and they are better than dried plants that seem to be so popular with florist shops. Choose ficus plants that have broad, rounded leaves. The money plant with its jade like succulent leaves is another excellent choice.

Avoid plants that have thorns. Thus bourganvilleas, while stunning in an office environment is unsuitable since it has thorns. And obviously cactus plants are a major taboo. I have seen friends of mine suffer from the most severe bad luck simply because they placed cute little cactus plants on their windowsill.

Cactus sends little slivers of bad energy which, when accumulated over a period of time cause misfortunes. When my friends removed their cactus plants, their problems soon got solved and their well being improved noticeably.

A painting of an acorn branch or any other fruit plant with fruits, when displayed in the Southeast is a wonderful symbol of prosperity luck.

The implied meaning of a rich harvest suggests success and prosperity.

CHAPTER
THREE

FENG SHUI
IN THE
OFFICE

LUCKY AND
UNLIKELY
OBJECTS

Place coins and bells on door knobs | TIP 81

When you use your coins and bells for feng shui purposes, you should always tie them together with red thread or red ribbon since this energizes the essence of their symbolic meanings. You can use ordinary copper coins but it best to use the old Chinese coins that have a square hole in the center.

COINS ON THE INSIDE

Coins tied together with red string should be placed on the inside of the door. This symbolizes that prosperity has already entered your office. If you place coins on the outside of the door, it denotes only a state of eventual prosperity, the promise of prosperity which could well NOT materialize. It is not necessary to put a hundred coins ! In feng shui more coins do not necessarily translate into a larger quantity of wealth luck. Three coins is sufficient. Do not place five coins as five is not a number that is conducive to wealth creation.

BELLS ON THE OUTSIDE

If you hang a pair of bells just outside your door, hanging on the doorknob, it attracts good fortune chi to enter your office. Symbolically the sound of bells announces the coming of prosperity and good news. Placing bells outside the office door, especially if your company, or the company you work for is engaged in trading, wholesale or retail business is an excellent feng shui feature.

Again it is not necessary to overdo things. Choose small bells made of metal if the main door is facing West, Northwest, or North. Do not use metal bells in the East and Southeast. Ceramic or crystal bells here and in the South, Southwest and Northeast would create more harmonious element energies and thus more auspicious.

Hang coins on door knob INSIDE the office

Hang a pair of bells OUTSIDE the door

CHAPTER
THREE

FENG SHUI
IN THE
OFFICE

LUCKY AND
UNLIKELY
OBJECTS

Element harmony in door design | TIP 82

    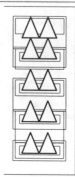

DOOR A	DOOR B	DOOR C	DOOR D	DOOR E
A door with **wood** element design	A door with **earth** element design	A door with **water** element design	A door with **metal** element design	A door with **fire** element design

Door designs can be made to harmonize perfectly with the direction they face, which often corresponds also with their location in the house layout. Thus if your main door faces the East or Southeast then Door A would be ideal since the rectangular design on the door indicates the growth element of wood, which in turn is the element of the East and Southeast. This design is also suitable for the South since wood produces fire in the Productive cycle.

If your main door is located in, or directly facing the West and Northwest, a door design that represents the metal element is auspicious. An example of this is shown above as Door D. Circular designs and shapes belong to the metal element. which is the reason moongates are often a feature along the West side of the garden of old Chinese family homes.

The water design or shape which is wavy is excellent for the north, itself a corner that symbolizes water. If your door faces north such a wavy design is also excellent. Water patterns are also excellent for doors that face East and Southeast. An example of a water design door is shown above as Door C.

The fire design door is perfect for doors that face South. The triangular pointed design (shown as Door E) is also excellent as a defensive type of door design that effectively blocks any *killing chi* that may be coming at the office. The fire design door is doubly excellent for people born in a fire year.

Finally the square earth design (Door B) is ideal for Northeast and Southwest.

CHAPTER
THREE

FENG SHUI
IN THE
OFFICE

LUCKY AND
UNLIKELY
OBJECTS

The luck implication of windows | TIP 83

Although windows are less important than doors in feng shui, it is productive to know about the luck implications in window design. This has to do with the shape that represents the different elements, the color. As well as where and how many windows there are. The windows into your office are places where the energy of the room also enters and leaves. It is secondary to the doors. Nevertheless windows that have good views and are designed to balance with spatial feng shui concepts bring greater harmony to the work place than windows that have not been planned in accordance to feng shui.

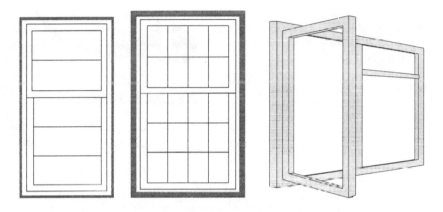

According to feng shui recommendations office windows <u>should open</u> outwards to symbolize a welcoming gesture to the good energy that floats in the outside environment. Feng shui stays silent on windows that slide open up/down. This point can thus be ignored.

The most important thing about the window is that it should not, at any time undermine the luck of your office. Thus the following guidelines about windows should be useful.

- There should not be too many windows. A ratio of three windows to every one door is sufficient.
- Windows should not occupy every wall in a room. The best configuration is that only two walls should have windows. When there are too many windows it represent loss of wealth, and loss of income.
- Windows should not be directly opposite the main door. *Chi* flies in and flies out again just as quickly. The effect is like having a mirror directly face the front door and that is inauspicious.
- Use element shapes to create harmony between the windows of your office with that of the five elements present in your personal space.

CHAPTER
THREE

FENG SHUI
IN THE
OFFICE

LUCKY AND
UNLIKELY
OBJECTS

Keep the Arrowana or feng shui fish | TIP 84

The Chinese of Malaysia, Singapore, Thailand and Indonesia are familiar with the magical qualities of the Arrowana – they refer to this river freshwater tropical fish as the feng shui fish, and business tycoons pay thousands for a full grown Arrowana. The scales of this fish are silver and they shimmer in shades of pink as an omen of good fortune.

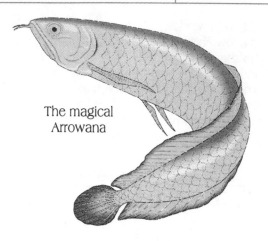

The magical Arrowana

Arrowanas are available in the UK and Europe for about forty pounds for a ten inch specimen. These fish grow to about a length of three feet.

Businessmen who keep them in the office usually have a huge aquarium that has nothing but water and the single Arrowana. There is no need to decorate the aquarium with water plants and sand. The Arrowana eats anything in sight. If you keep this fish, feed it fresh river worms or small goldfish to bring out the valuable. pink glow.
If you use specially packed fish food, get the best. Unless your Arrowana looks good it will not bring you wealth luck. And keep it either in the North, East or Southeast of your office. Do not have an oversize tank !

My Five Arrowanas

In 1987, I installed a large aquarium in the living room of my apartment on the Peak in Hong Kong. I knew I would have to restructure my life if I were to be able to spend enough time with Jennifer. And I also knew that to stop working I had to make enough money to retire. I turned to feng shui and bought five Arrowanas from a Hong Kong pet shop.
I fed my Arrowanas a diet of live goldfish to bring out the pink glow. My Arrowana's scales glimmered in a range of red, gold and pink colors! They were beautiful!

In eighteen months they grew from 10 inches to 18 inches. In that same time I also succeeded in my game plan. I made enough to stop working and to return home to Malaysia.

I was offered HK$300,000 for my Arrowanas but released them instead into the Stanley reservoir. Each fish circled three times in front of me before swimming into the depths of the reservoir!

CHAPTER
THREE

FENG SHUI
IN THE
OFFICE

LUCKY AND
UNLIKELY
OBJECTS

Be wary of the *art* you hang | TIP 85

I have seen the most wonderful feng shui art hanging in corporate offices and I have also seen some horrendous examples. Interior decorators who develop an *eye* for good feng shui art will serve their clients a lot better since the result will not only be pleasing, it will also create auspicious good luck as well. Here are some feng shui ground rules on hanging art in the office.

- Generally <u>avoid abstract art</u> that has too many sharp edges and whose colors clash with the elements on the wall upon which they are hung. Art that suggests metal could be harmful when hung on the East or Southeast.
- Also avoid so called *character or intellectual art* that show wizened old men or art that record the tragedies of our age. These can set up negative vibrations that can translate into bad luck. If you want to hang portraits of the monarch, or the founder of your company, the best place corner is the Northwest wall. Hung here, the painting becomes transformed into a potent feng shui tool and it activates the luck of the magnificent trigram *chien.*
- The best art to have in the office is landscape art. Feng shui is about the landscape, and if you can it into the office in a way which does not create imbalance, you will enjoy harmonious feng shui. A good rule of thumb is to place a mountain painting behind you and have a water feature in front of you. A carpet of flowers in a field in front of you is also excellent as this symbolizes the bright hall.
- Paintings of flowers and fruits are also good feng shui, but it is not a good idea to hang peonies and other flowers that signify romance. Better to hang· paintings of fruits, and these are best hung on walls on the East Side.
- Paintings of fish can often create wonderful feng shui energies but be very wary of paintings of wild animals. The tiger, the leopard, the lion – these magnificent cats can sometimes cause problems.

Carp is always auspicious.
A garden scene with a
curved stepping pathway
symbolizes progress.

A painting with the good fortune character
"*fook*" which means luck shown above is
excellent feng shui.

CHAPTER
THREE

FENG SHUI
IN THE
OFFICE

LUCKY AND
UNLIKELY
OBJECTS

Keep trash bins out of sight

TIP 86

All cleaning gear – brooms and dust pans are deemed to symbolize bad luck, and must be kept out of sight of the entire office, and especially the main door.

The connotation here is that the presence of the broom in the vicinity of the foyer area *sweeps out all your good fortune.* Brooms are thus regarded as anathema to feng shui. Keep them inside cleaning closets or storerooms.

The TRASH BIN
Should be kept out of sight too, and preferably it should be covered. Place your trash basket under your table where it is not visible from the main door, or the door into your private office (if you have one).

If you are paranoid about security, a popular feng shui method of keeping unwanted visitors and troublemakers from coming into your office is to place a broom upside down just outside your entrance door each time the office is kept locked. Usually this will be evening time and during the weekends. Do not leave your broom there during working hours since the broom will *sweep all your business visitors away.*

A broom placed upside down just outside the entrance door keeps out unwanted visitors. It is also good for security luck.

The broom outside the door really does keep people from visiting your office. Since this is what you need to do for the nights and for weekends apply this recommendation then.

BUT do not forget to remove the broom each morning when you come to work.

CHAPTER
FOUR

FENG SHUI
TO BOOST
YOUR
CAREER

IMPROVE
YOUR
CHANCES
OF
SUCCESS

Activating your career luck | TIP 87

If you are have serious ambitions to make it big in your career, you can use feng shui to give your ambitions a boost. Good career feng shui usually manifests in the form of increased opportunities. It will make you a much busier person, so unless you are prepared to grab new opportunities that come your way, the benefits will be limited. It is important to realize this, otherwise you could well feel hassled by the sudden new scope your working life now takes. Those of you who are workaholics however will benefit tremendously when you activate your career luck. Your hard work will start to reap dividends. Powerful bosses will notice you within your work place, and extra responsibilities will be heaped upon your shoulders. You will start to operate in a different league.

When I energized my career luck, it took off so fast I did not know if I was coming or going. That was in the year 1982, a year I made so many quantum leaps in my career, it scared me. So when you start energizing your career luck do be prepared to be surprised.

THE CAREER CORNER

Is the <u>North</u> of any residential building or personal space. Thus to get the most out of career feng shui you should use feng shui methods to energize the NORTH corner of both your home, as well as your office.

<u>AT home</u>, if the north corner is your bedroom, do not do anything inside the bedroom. Instead you can activate the north corner of your living room. If the north corner of your home is where you have the toilet, the consequences are inauspicious for the careers of residents. Close the toilet, and if you can, try not to use it. The way to overcome the negative effect of the toilet is to place a big boulder in side to press down of the bad *chi* caused by the toilet.

Have a small aquarium filled with guppies in the NORTH wall or corner of both your living room at home, and in your office.

Your aquarium should not be more than two feet lengthwise. I recommend guppies because these small fish are hardy little creatures with stunning tail fins. They create good yang energy because they swim vigorously.

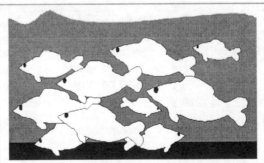

Get a whole school of guppies or other lively active fish and watch them swim strongly, creating strong career luck for you.

CHAPTER
FOUR

FENG SHUI
TO BOOST
YOUR
CAREER

IMPROVE
YOUR
CHANCES
OF
SUCCESS

Success luck with feng shui doors

TIP 88

A door with glass panel as shown is usually <u>not</u> recommended. Doors should always be solid. The design on the door itself should be in accordance with the element of the location of the door.

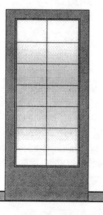

Try to avoid having sliding doors opening into your office, or into your study at home. Doors should always open inwards to be auspicious

Doors should be solid and firm to be auspicious. Doors should also be large enough to comfortably accommodate the occupant of the room.

Career luck is much improved when the location, direction and design of the door that enters into your private office is designed according to feng shui principles. It is not possible to get everything correct but you should endeavour to observe some of the major taboos.

Start by making sure your door is not being hit by anything harmful. These are sharp edges, long corridors, exposed beams, corners and pillars.

Next try to have your door located in a corner of your room, and facing a direction that is auspicious to you. If your door cannot face your best direction, at least make sure it is not facing your *chueh ming* or total loss direction. This is regarded as a major feature to observe.

Avoid putting glass panels on your door. Transparent glass is more harmful than opaque glass but both are to be avoided. Select door designs that are harmonious with the element of the corner in which it is located. (see Tip 82), and if you like, you can even paint your door according to element indications.
<u>Browns</u> for East and Southeast; <u>White</u> for West and Northwest; <u>Maroon</u> for South; <u>Blacks</u> for North and Beige for Southwest and Northeast.

CHAPTER
FOUR

FENG SHUI
TO BOOST
YOUR
CAREER

IMPROVE
YOUR
CHANCES
OF
SUCCESS

Sitting in your power position | TIP 89

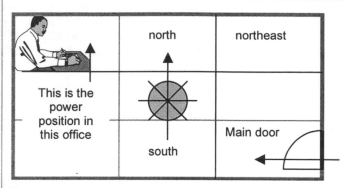

	north	northeast
This is the power position in this office	south	Main door

The power position in any office is the corner that is diagonally opposite the main door. It is deep inside the office. Try to sit in this spot to get the best career luck.

Guidelines on sitting in the power position

- Inside your personal office , continue to maintain the opposite corner diagonal guideline for the placement of your desk.
- Sit facing the door. Never have your back to the door. For career people this will mean you losing out in any politicking. It also means your subordinates will betray you, and you have a hard time managing them.
- Sit with a solid wall behind you. Do not have the window behind you. Do not have the any door behind you.
- Sit with more space in front of you than behind you. If possible have at least a minimum of three feet of space in front of you. This simulates a small space for good fortune to accumulate in front of you.
- Sit with windows on your left or in front of you.

Note: To activate the NORTH corner of your house or office it is important to take your directions correctly. I have been asked many times "how do we determine the career corner" and when I tell them it is the North corner of their office, they then ask me *how* they should determine where the North is. I had not been aware that in some schools of feng shui, the North is deemed to be in the sector where the door is located. This is incorrect.

The North, (or any corner) of a body of enclosed space is where the compass needle points to. In feng shui we speak of the magnetic North as opposed to the true north. So invest in a good compass, and then, standing in approximately the center of your office, note where the needle points to. To demarcate the North (and other) sectors of your office, divide your office floor area into nine equal grids, as shown above. It is then a simple enough matter to identify the North sector.

CHAPTER
FOUR

FENG SHUI
TO BOOST
YOUR
CAREER

IMPROVE
YOUR
CHANCES
OF
SUCCESS

Desk shapes and placement

TIP 90

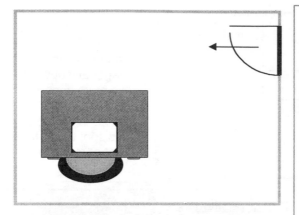

Back table/ cabinet
like this is excellent

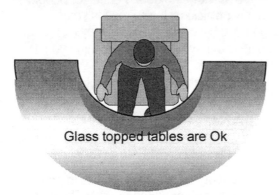

Glass topped tables are Ok

This desk arrangement is shaped like a semi circle and *embraces* the occupant. It is a very popular feature in desk design and is usually custom-made. Desks like these are acceptable from a feng shui perspective are acceptable if the curve is not too wide as to resemble a knife cutting into the occupant. They can also be made of glass in which case the edges should be properly smoothed out.

Place a regular rectangular shaped desk diagonally opposite the entrance door. Orientate the sitting direction according to your good directions but make sure you face the door. If there is a beam above, move the desk out of its way.

Do not have an L shaped, or a U shaped table as these are considered inauspicious from a feng shui viewpoint.

Desks are usually made of wood and this is excellent. Some business tycoons I know opt for glass topped office desks and these are acceptable as long as they are West group people. If they are East group people glass tops are unsuitable.

Elaborately carved desks are also very auspicious. Chinese rose wood desks that have dragon carvings are believed to be especially auspicious. If you can afford such tables I strongly recommend them since they create wonderful success and prosperity symbolism. Mother of pearl in laid desks is also auspicious.

CHAPTER
FOUR

FENG SHUI
TO BOOST
YOUR
CAREER

IMPROVE
YOUR
CHANCES
OF
SUCCESS

Directions for business travel | TIP 91

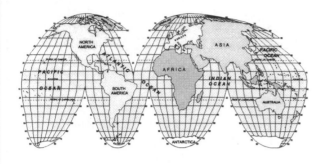

Look at the map of the world here. When routing your business travel note the direction of your travel. See what direction you are *travelling from* and travelling to !

Using your KUA number to determine your travel feng shui

FIRSTLY: go to page two and note your best and worst directions according to the Compass school formula. The rule to note is that you will get excellent feng shui luck in your travel and business trips if you travel FROM one of your best directions. Please note that it is the direction you travel from that is important, not the direction you are travelling to. Many people have got this interpretation wrong; even my feng shui Master himself got it wrong for many years until he checked the classical old text again to make certain we got everything correct for my book on this particular formula.

SECONDLY: if you are an EAST group person, then you know that travelling towards the West is generally favorable since then you are flying *from* the East, thereby bringing good luck with you where you are going.
If you a WEST group person, then the opposite holds true. You are better off travelling towards the East.

Example: If you live in the UK and you are an East group person, and you have to make a business trip to Hong Kong, you will not be flying with feng shui luck since you would be flying from the direction NORTHWEST which is one of your bad directions. This travel direction is suitable for a West group person. For those making the journey the other way, i.e. from Hong Kong to the UK, the travel direction is Southeast, which is suitable for an East group person, because this is an auspicious direction for an East group person.

THIRDLY: This aspect of feng shui practice is applicable for travel within a country or within a city. If you travel to work everyday *from* a direction that is auspicious for you, your *going to work feng shui route* would be better than if you went to work using a route that is inauspicious for you.

CHAPTER
FOUR

FENG SHUI
TO BOOST
YOUR
CAREER

IMPROVE
YOUR
CHANCES
OF
SUCCESS

Recognition luck with feng shui | TIP 92

There is no greater boost to careers than for one's efforts, skill and expertise to be acknowledged and recognized by someone in authority. Indeed, *luck* has often been described as being in the right place at the right time. All this means is that if one has the luck, one will surely catch the eye of someone who is in a position to enlarge one's responsibilities based on the exactly this recognition.

Feng shui works wonders in enhancing this type of luck. Throughout my career days, every piece of work I did, often got recognized and acknowledged so that my climb up the career ladder was peppered with gratifying instances of recognition. Those were heady days indeed.

So let me share ONE career tip on getting recognized. Remember it is not enough to be hardworking and clever. Almost everyone has some skills to speak of and many people work very hard yet never get recognized. One must be perceived as success material. Only then can one's attributes get translated into promotions, higher income, more responsibilities and so forth. This requires luck, and feng shui can often provide this kind of luck.

A QUARTZ CRYSTAL
ON YOUR TABLE

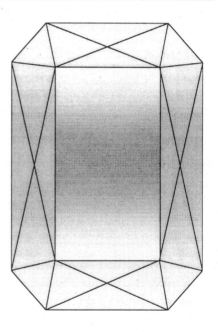

All through my working life I placed a very large rectangular cut crystal made by Tiffany's on my desk top. This is sketched out on the right. I chose a rectangular shape because this represents the wood element which was beneficial for me. It was also in harmony with the *celestial dragon* of the East, whose element was also wood.

I placed this crystal on the left-hand side of my desk and often used it as a paperweight. The combined energies created by the intrinsic earth essence of the crystal and by the wood element that represented growth were most beneficial. You can do the same.

CHAPTER
FOUR

FENG SHUI
TO BOOST
YOUR
CAREER

IMPROVE
YOUR
CHANCES
OF
SUCCESS

Energizing the feng shui of your files | TIP 93

Energize all your important files with prosperity coins that symbolize good fortune. The key to activating these coins is the red ribbon used to tie the coins together

It is not necessary to energize all your files. Only the important ones that contain letters and documents connected with your work and your business. I energize all my INCOME files as well as my Investments files. This helps to create prosperity energies for the success of my work, and to date this method has not failed me.

THE METHOD
You will need the Chinese coins that have a square hole in the center. Take three of these coins and tie them together, *yang* side up, either with a red ribbon or with red thread. The *yang* side is the side that has four instead of two characters. Tape the coins onto the cover of your files with strong cellophane tape, checking occasionally to make sure the coins do not fall off.

OTHER GUIDELINES ON PROTECTING THE FENG SHUI OF YOUR FILES

- Never allow your important files to be stepped upon. Thus you should never place them on the floor no matter how busy you are or how cluttered your office gets. When your files get stepped upon it creates extreme negative energy that affects your work luck.
- Never allow your important files to be placed under the table either. This also has the same bad effect.
- Never allow your important files to be placed under staircases. This means that filing cabinets must not be under staircases.
- Never place files next to a toilet. Again filing cabinets should not be placed against a wall with a toilet on the other side.

CHAPTER
FOUR

FENG SHUI
TO BOOST
YOUR
CAREER

IMPROVE
YOUR
CHANCES
OF
SUCCESS

Pressing down the nasty *five yellows* | TIP 94

Each year, it is vital to note where the nasty "*five yellows*" has flown. This part of time dimension feng shui must be taken care of if you are to have career and prosperity success. The five yellows cause misfortunes to occur in the form of losses, setbacks, bad health and accidents.

The table on the right here spells out the location of the five yellows over the next twelve years. This means that every year the afflicted direction/location changes, and you would be most well advised to take note of this at the start of each lunar new year

In 1998, the afflicted direction is the NORTHEAST . Thus the bad luck of this part of the house and office must be nullified if you are to have good luck. The best way to do this is to use a metal windchime to press down on the bad luck of the five yellows.

Windchimes used for this purpose should preferably have five solid rods . This creates a more melodious sound. Also, because the use of the windchime is not to channel chi upwards, it is not necessary to have windchimes with hollow rods. Thus in 1998 hang just such a windchime in the Northeast part of your house.

It would be ideal of course if the toilet or kitchen were in the place or corner of the home that houses the *five yellows.* For instance if there is a toilet in the Northeast, the house will enjoy better luck in 1998 since the toilet would have effectively pressed down on the *5 yellows bad luck* of the Northeast. This notwithstanding, it would also help to hang the windchime

YEAR	LOCATION of the *FIVE YELLOWS*
1998	Northeast
1999	South
2000	North
2001	Southwest
2002	West
2002	Southeast
2003	Center
2004	Northwest
2005	West
2006	Northeast
2007	South
2008	North
2009	Southwest

A five rod windchime

The tinkling sounds of the windchimes is supposed to represent the sound of tiger cubs that serve to divert the attention of the "Tiger" thereby preventing the Tiger from turning malevolent !

CHAPTER
FOUR

FENG SHUI
TO BOOST
YOUR
CAREER

IMPROVE
YOUR
CHANCES
OF
SUCCESS

Do not sit next to, or below toilets

TIP 95

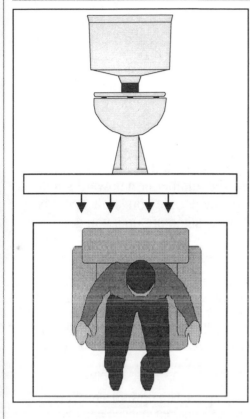

Go and check whether you are sitting directly below a toilet on the floor above you ! This is an especially harmful situation in the office, and you should move your desk away from under the toilet immediately.

At home, if you have a study or work room on your ground level, make certain there is no toilet directly above you.

It is equally important to make sure you do not *share* a wall with a toilet. If the toilet occupies a room next to your study and the toilet itself is located on the other wall the situation is not harmful. It is only when you actually share a wall with a toilet that you should move your desk away.

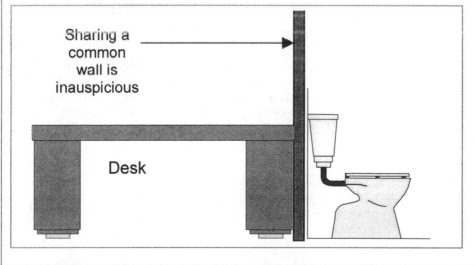

Sharing a common wall is inauspicious

Desk

CHAPTER
FOUR

FENG SHUI
TO BOOST
YOUR
CAREER

IMPROVE
YOUR
CHANCES
OF
SUCCESS

The Prosperity signature   TIP 96

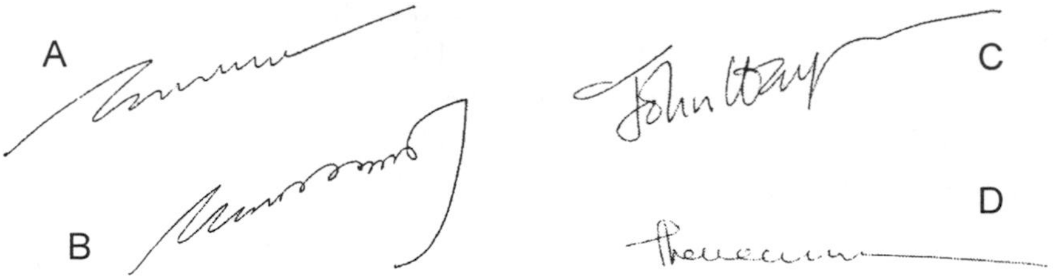

A signature is said to attract great prosperity and success if it starts
with a firm upward stroke and ends with another firm upward stroke.
Check out the signatures of the successful people you know and when
you are convinced, practice your new signature until you get it.

SIGNATURE A
From a feng shui perspective this will be the most auspicious signature of the
four shown here. Note the upward starting stroke, and the upward ending
stroke. This denotes a good beginning and a good ending to every project and
job undertaken. My feng shui master tells me If you sign this type of signature
forty nine times on a wish list for forty nine days, your wishes will come true !

SIGNATURE B
This signature is only partly correct. It starts with a firm upward stroke but it
ends with an equally firm downward stroke. Signatures that seem to end with
a backward movement are not auspicious. It indicates a sad ending.

SIGNATURE C
This is another example of a signature that has excellent feng shui. Once again
note that the beginning stroke is upward and the ending stroke is also upward.
An ending upward stroke, which is a line under the signature, is also regarded
as part of the signature. Thus those of you who do not have an upward
ending stroke could include a firm line upwards to create the prosperity
signature.

SIGNATURE D
This signature has an almost unnoticeable downward slant to its ending. It is
therefore not auspicious. If your signature looks like this, try to change it so the
stroke is moving upwards.

CHAPTER
FOUR

FENG SHUI
TO BOOST
YOUR
CAREER

IMPROVE
YOUR
CHANCES
OF
SUCCESS

The feng shui of watches and clocks | TIP 97

 The Chinese are so *pantang* or deadly averse to, receiving watches and clocks as gifts. In fact the older the recipient the more aggravated he or she becomes when a clock is given as a birthday gift.
This is because the timepiece is regarded as symbolizing the negative effects of time.

The clock, more than any other object represents the passing of time. It is the antithesis of longevity symbols. As such, clocks are regarded as being extremely inauspicious objects around the office. I remember years ago in Hong Kong when I nearly bought myself an antique grandfather clock for the office, which I thought exhibited "so much character" my feng shui expert friend strongly advised against the purchase. *Very bad for business* he said !

He told me that feng shui masters have attributed the fall of the Qing dynasty in China to the great many clocks the Qing rulers received as gifts from the Western emissaries. These foreign visitors paid their respects at the Chinese Court and almost always brought along an elaborate European clock as a gift. No wonder all the young Princes died! Indeed I myself have seen entire rooms full of these bejeweled clocks on display inside special rooms in the Forbidden City.

A WATCH AS A GIFT ...

If you receive a watch as a gift, especially if it is a birthday gift, you should thank whoever gave it to you but immediately offer a token dollar coin to nullify any negative effects. This symbolizes that you have immediately "purchased' the watch from whoever gave it to you. According to advice given to me, it is perfectly acceptable for parents to give watches to their children as gifts BUT not the other way around.

Children should never give watches to their parents, grand parents or any of the older members of the family since this strongly signifies the passage of time. Symbolically therefore they are the opposite of long life symbols like peaches and bamboo, the crane and the deer. When you present an elder of the family with a watch, no matter how special and expensive it is, your gift will not be regarded favourably, Better to stick to the more traditional gifts like a painting of bamboo or a statue of the God of longevity.

CHAPTER
FOUR

FENG SHUI
TO BOOST
YOUR
CAREER

TIPS FOR
PERSONAL
GROOMING

Dress according to your five elements | TIP 98

Personalized feng shui has to do with the personal elements that rule our birth chart and these are usually viewed as a basket of elements in accordance with our *four pillars*. Another way of expressing the four pillars is our *eight characters*. This is because each *pillar* has *two characters* which thus make up a total of eight. Chinese fortune telling is always referred to in terms of one's 8 characters or *paht chee*. I seldom refer to my full four pillars *paht chee* chart simply because it is too complicated to work out. It is also because I have found that using the KUA numbers to identify the elements that work best for me is as equally effective as using the *paht chee* method. Refer to page 1 and 2 to work out your KUA number and then look at the table below and note the shapes that will enhance your different types of luck. Incorporate the rectangular, square, round, wavy or triangular shapes into the cut of your clothes as well as the patterns and prints you select for your ties, your shirts and so forth.

- Stripes are excellent for those whose best shapes are rectangular.
- Triangles and A line dresses are of the fire element
- Square shapes denote the earth element
- Round shapes and circles are of the metal element
- Wavy shapes represent the water element.

Personalized feng shui can also be guided by the elements that are symbolized by our body shape, which change as we age. Thus determine the shape that best describes YOU and then dress according to the productive cycle of the elements. Thus if your body shape is triangular i.e. small on top and heavy at the bottom then dressing with the rectangular shape in mind is excellent since wood (rectangle) produces fire (triangular).

Your KUA number	1	2	3	4	5	6	7	8	9
Your *success* Shape	▪ stripes	■	▲	⬳	■ square	●	●	■	▪
Your *good health* shape	▪ stripes	●	⬳ zigzag	▲ A line	● round	■ checks	■	●	▪
Your *romance* shape	▲ A line	●	▪	▪	●	■	■	●	⬳
Your *attractive* shape	⬳ wavy	■	▪	▪	■	● circle	●	■	▲

CHAPTER
FOUR

FENG SHUI
TO BOOST
YOUR
CAREER

TIPS FOR
PERSONAL
GROOMING

Balancing Elements with shapes | TIP 99

Good feng shui in personal grooming can be achieved by skillfully balancing the elements that make up the total *look*. Combining shapes and colors in a way that ensure the elements stay in harmony can do this, The examples summarized on this page offer ideas for other combinations.

- A rounded hairstyle on a rectangular shaped face indicates metal on wood. This would be inauspicious.
- A rounded hairstyle on a oval or heart shaped face indicates metal above fire. Very inauspicious
- A rounded hairstyle on a square face (as shown in the sketch) represents metal above earth. This would be a lot better since earth produces metal. This would then be an auspicious combination.

- Long wavy hair always suggests the water motif. If your body shape is long and tall, then the element combinations suggest water and wood – a most auspicious combination as the elements are in harmony.
- Long wavy hair (water element) matched with a suit in blue, purple or black would mean too much water. The effect would then be imbalance, and the feng shui is not great!
- If your body frame tends to be short and stocky, then wearing a straight tailored suit as shown suggests an excess of the earth element since the overall shape is square. It would help if the suit is white (metal) since the combination or earth and metal would then be very auspicious.

Good feng shui in dressing always means good element harmony. The way to ensure you get this right is to look in the mirror and to pick out at least three items that represent element harmony. From the shape and texture of your hairstyle to the cut of your clothes, the colors and the patterns of your outfit you will be able to form an impression that seems harmonious or not. Develop your *eye* and it soon becomes part of you !

CHAPTER
FOUR

FENG SHUI
TO BOOST
YOUR
CAREER

TIPS FOR
PERSONAL
GROOMING

Avoid combining elements destructively | TIP 100

It is always a good idea to memorize the element or elements that can harm you or which are discordant with your KUA number, or with your body shape. Sometimes when you check these various methods and formulas, it is possible that under one method, the element wood (rectangular, green) may be good for you and under another method it may be bad for you. When faced with such apparently contradictory indications, develop sensitivity to your own experience. Over time you will be able to isolate your good and bad colors, hairstyles and cuts.

For instance, I am a wood person because I was born in the year of wood. So green has ALWAYS done wonders for me. Theoretically fire would not be good for me since fire burns wood. But I was a winter wood because I was born in the month of January, sorely in need of heat and warmth. I discovered that if I wanted high energy level all I needed to do was dress in red. It never failed me. Red made me bloom and blossom. Apart from being a yang color it complemented my personal feng shui needs perfectly.

You should thus attempt to undertake your own personal element analysis this way. Check against your KUA number to determine the colors that are harmful for you and then experiment. Thus if yellow (bright yellow is fire and light yellow is earth element) is bad for you, try wearing it and see how the day goes for you. Do the same with prints and patterns, shapes and hairstyles.

Often, even if a color, shape or pattern by itself, may not be auspicious for you, the way you combine the elements in your total look can transform something bad into something good. Thus when in doubt, undertake the element analysis I suggested earlier. Let the elements in your grooming harmonize with each other.

In personal feng shui everything you wear has element symbolism and connotations. The man above is medium built suggesting metal energy in his body build. The color of his suit, his tie, his briefcase, his shoes also have element symbolism. Also note how much gold he is wearing (his cufflinks and other items of jewelry). Identify the whole basket of elements and then note if anything is missing, if there is too much of any element or if the combinations of the elements represented are destructive.

CHAPTER
FOUR

FENG SHUI
TO BOOST
YOUR
CAREER

TIPS FOR
PERSONAL
GROOMING

Pattern and color combinations — TIP 101

Denoting the wood element

STRIPES
- Are extremely lucky when done in all shades of reds and maroon;
- Are very unlucky when done in metallic colors or in white.
- Are very lucky when the background color is blue or black.
- White stripes on blue are lucky; white stripes on gold or silver are bad.
- Green stripes on darker green is excessive wood. Not good.
- Green stripes on black or blue is excellent.
- Green stripes on red denote success.

WAVY (water)   **DOTS** (metal)   **ZIGZAG** (fire)   **SQUARES** (earth)

WAVY LINES
- Balance well with blues and greens.
- Also excellent against a white background
- Clashes with bright reds and orange.
- Mixes well with dots and circles.
- Also goes well with rectangular shapes.

DOTS
- Are best done in metallic colors, gold, silvers and white.
- Very auspicious on a beige or earthy background.

ZIG ZAG lines
- Matches well with orange, beige and browns
- Are most auspicious on a background of green or brown.

SQUARES and CHECKS
- Matches extremely well with reds and yellows.
- Matches well also with whites and metallic colors
- Very inauspicious on a blue or black background.
- Not recommended in greens or blues.

CHAPTER
FOUR

FENG SHUI
TO BOOST
YOUR
CAREER

TIPS FOR
PERSONAL
GROOMING

Dirty, torn clothes create negative vibes | TIP 102

Dress like a hobo – with cut outs and torn shirts – and you soon turn into one !

One of the worst things anyone can do to undermine his or her feng shui is to wear dirty, torn clothes. Dressing like a hippie with hastily ripped out holes in your jeans, or going for the washed out faded look may well make you look cool with the younger *hip* generation. But old fashioned Chinese like me will frown strenuously on this kind of dressing. Why ? Simply because it brings such enormous bad luck.

Dressing like a hobo attracts poverty and bad luck vibrations that often translate into the most severe kind of ill fortune. My nephew and niece used to wear jeans with enormous cut outs ... and they had severe bad luck indeed ! When I saw these offensive jeans on them I strenuously advised them to get rid of them and to change their whole attitude towards dressing. They have since thrown out all their shirts with cut outs, and repaired all torn buttons. Their luck has improved.

BEING PROPERLY DRESSED BRINGS GOOD FENG SHUI.

Even when you have no plans to go out and even if you work from home, you should make sure that you never wear clothes that suggest that you are a slouch. As soon as you are ready to wake up and face the day, get out of your pajamas! Get out of your *sarong*!

Take the trouble to change your clothes, wear your make up and stay well groomed ready to greet in any good fortune that may come your way that very day ! Spray some scent. When you smell good, look good and feel good, your feng shui will likewise be so good too !

Wearing unflattering clothes create unflattering energies. Such clothes deplete you of yang energy and cause you to feel lethargic and lacking in energy. Change out of your sleep clothes as soon as you wake up, and do throw out those shapeless, unflattering so called *home clothes* !

CHAPTER
FOUR

FENG SHUI
TO BOOST
YOUR
CAREER

TIPS FOR
PERSONAL
GROOMING

Good grooming makes good feng shui | TIP 103

Being well groomed does not necessarily mean dressing to the heights of fashion. It does not mean dressing in designer clothes. Good grooming does not have to be expensive. Good grooming means presenting a balanced, harmonious look to the world. It means having clothes that have fluid lines, that look neat and are clean. All the guidelines for arranging one's space harmoniously apply with equal emphasis to one's appearance. And, as with space feng shui, good grooming feng shui also calls for balance and harmony.

Here are two important tips that apply to the feng shui of appearance.

THE FENG SHUI OF WEARING JEWELLERY

Whether you wear the real thing or the fabulous fakes, please remember that jewelry represent an excellent and most harmonious combination. This is because the combination of the earth (**stones**) and the metal elements (**gold, platinum and silver**) reflect the productive cycle of the elements.

Wearing jewelry, and especially gold jewelry that is set with precious stones (diamonds, rubies, sapphires and emeralds) does represent excellent feng shui. So I usually encourage people to use accessories as adornments to one's appearance. But you should not overdo things. If you end up looking like a Christmas tree, the effect could be an excess of metal, The resulting imbalance of the elements then becomes harmful, and is especially injurious to those born during the spring months and in years that are of the wood element. Too much gold kills *wood* born people !

THE FENG SHUI OF BEING SLIGHTLY PLUMP

It is also better to look slightly prosperous and have some flesh than to look thin and scrawny. To the Chinese, being <u>too thin</u> is the surest indicator of bad luck. By the same token being just a tiny bit over weight (not flabby but full) is usually regarded as looking, and being prosperous. Rich Chinese women who are first wives (called *tai tais)* are usually a little plump, as opposed to courtesans and concubines who are usually thin. Meanwhile, rich Chinese men almost always have a tummy. These are highly valued indicators of prosperity.

CHAPTER
FOUR

FENG SHUI
TO BOOST
YOUR
CAREER

TIPS FOR
PERSONAL
GROOMING

Wearing and carrying accessories | TIP 104

handbag

Feng shui grooming takes account of the accessories you carry and wear since these add to your total look.

HANDBAGS
Ladies who carry handbags (or pocket books as they are called in the United States) can select them using feng shui knowledge to enhance their feng shui significance. Use the two standard benchmarks – shape and color · to check the element combination on the bag. This should indicate if the bag has good or bad energy and therefore whether it has good feng shui. Thus:

Rectangular in browns, blacks and greens are good.
Squares in beige, maroons, reds and yellows are good.
Circulars in white, and beige are good.

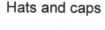

buttons

BUTTONS
Buttons are usually round and when these are made of a metallic medium represents strong metal element. Such buttons would be excellent for those wearing black or blue; but most inauspicious for those wearing greens and browns. Plastic round buttons are basically harmonious.

Hats and caps

HATS and CAPS
Head covers signify shelter and are generally regarded as good feng shui. But hats and caps should not be black or blue in color. This represents the water element for the head – which in feng shui is supposedly most inauspicious. *Water above mountain* is one of the four danger indications of the I Ching. The great Masters of feng shui interpret this to signify the danger of having the water element on the head, and on the roof.

TIES and SCARVES
These accessories have no feng shui significance except in the colors and patterns that are printed on them. Use the color guides to apply element analysis to the wearing of ties and scarves.

ties

CHAPTER
FOUR

FENG SHUI
TO BOOST
YOUR
CAREER

TIPS FOR
PERSONAL
GROOMING

Create facial balance with make up | TIP 105

Chinese matriarchs are great believers in the science of *face reading*, and would usually be reluctant for their sons to marry women whose faces indicated bad luck for their husbands.

Bad luck faces were described as:

- Faces that did not have enough flesh; thus sunken cheekbones and the gaunt look popularized by the super thin super models were usually dismissed as bad.

- Faces that had too wide a jaw – to the extent that it looked angular. (like Jackie Kennedy) Square jawed women were believed to eat their husbands. This is translated to mean that their husbands would die at a young age, or at any rate long before them. In the old days, such women would usually have a hard time finding husbands from good families.

- Faces whose eyes are too close together. Such faces are deemed to be *poverty* faces. Those with this kind of face are believed to have hardships, as they grow older. In other words their early life is better than their old age.

- If a face has thick eyebrows, it would be considered even more negatively. Thin and well-shaped eyebrows are usually preferred and regarded more favourably than bushy eyebrows. Eyebrows should thus be trimmed and plucked to look less bushy.

USING MAKE UP
TO IMPROVE FACIAL BALANCE

In feng shui, what you perceive, i.e. what you actually see, is what is important. Thus it is possible to use make up to correct features that are deemed to be bad feng shui.

- Firstly make sure faces are well balanced. Do not go for the high cheekbones so enamoured by the Western concept of beauty. *Holes in the cheeks* are deemed to be bad feng shui. To be prosperous cheeks must look full, luscious. And prosperous.

- Lips must be small but full.

- Noses should be high, round and fleshy. The more fleshy the nose is the more prosperity you will have !

- Jaws should be full. Small inadequate jaws indicate a short life.

CHAPTER
FOUR

FENG SHUI
TO BOOST
YOUR
CAREER

TIPS FOR
PERSONAL
GROOMING

The feng shui of your dressing table | TIP 106

To start with, always sit facing one of your four good directions when applying your face make up.

This means that as you stare at yourself in the mirror, you are staring into a direction that represents one of your auspicious directions according to the KUA formula. Not only will this bring you luck as you put on your *face* in the mornings, it will also put in a most pleasant frame of mind.

LIGHTING
THE DRESSING TABLE

The best feng shui feature at a dressing table is to have the presence of a bright light. This brings yang energy and also suggests the fire element. This brings a great deal of auspicious energy to your daily grooming ritual. If your dressing table is located in the South, Southwest or Northeast of your bedroom, this lighting feature will be even more auspicious.

Always make sure that your dressing table does not have its mirror directly facing your bed.

This creates bad feng shui for you when you are sleeping. If you have to have the dressing table inside your bedroom, try to make sure the mirror is placed in a way that does not reflect the bed. If it does, the mirror will bring you grief.

A mirror facing the bed is often the cause of a happy marriage going sour. You could suffer from problems caused by the entrance of one or more outside third party coming into the relationship. If you presently have a mirror facing your bed, cover the mirror at night with a table cloth or reposition your dressing table.

bed

This arrangement is acceptable. The mirror is NOT directly reflecting the bed.

CHAPTER
FOUR

FENG SHUI
TO BOOST
YOUR
CAREER

TIPS FOR
PERSONAL
GROOMING

The feng shui of facial enhancement | TIP 107

Having bright red cheeks on a fair colored countenance is almost always considered a face of good fortune. In the old days when make up was less freely available, various herbal concoctions brought color to the cheeks, lips and eyes of the young women of marriageable age.

<u>Rosy cheeks</u> symbolized the promise of fertility, which in women was regarded as great good fortune. Rosy cheeks that were full and rounded were viewed as being even better fortune. Such cheeks indicate a life that gets better and more prosperous. Thus the modern day use of cheek color is an excellent feng shui practice which I thoroughly encourage.

<u>A fair complexion</u> that had no blemishes was also considered a face of good fortune. Moles, freckles and other unsightly birthmarks were usually frowned upon as indicating obstacles in one's life. Moles at the back of the neck were especially frowned upon since this indicated a hard life with a burden to carry.

Marks (including moles) on any part of the face, but especially along the center line were considered indicators of hardships at various times of the person's life. Young women often got rid of these moles and freckles to enhance both their appearance as well as their good fortune. The covering sticks of modern make up today can do the job less painfully!

<u>Good fortune lips</u> are supposed to be tiny and very red. Women who had naturally bright lips that were also small and dainty were highly regarded as great beauties and women of great good fortune. Large thick lips were considered a sign of poverty and represented a certain hardship in life. I hasten to add that I personally adore full lush lips despite this feng shui belief.

The Chinese believed that a woman's face offered signs of her good or bad fortune. In the old days, the art of face reading was often applied when checking out prospective daughters in law. And according to feng shui good fortune was indicated by good coloring, fullness of figure and firmness of flesh – these are attributes that can be achieved quite easily in today's world.

Good luck faces are usually round and rather plump. The jaw line should not be too wide since this indicates early widowhood.

Hair should be combed well back and adorned with gold ornaments. Hair that is parted in the center indicated a life devoid of family. A well-adorned head attracts good fortune to a woman's family.

107

CHAPTER
FOUR

FENG SHUI
TO BOOST
YOUR
CAREER

TIPS FOR
PERSONAL
GROOMING

Never hang washing out overnight | TIP 108

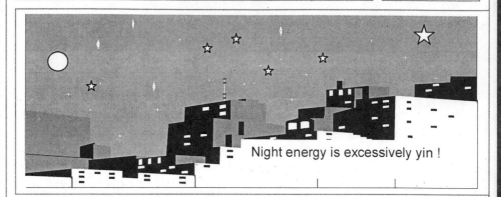

Night energy is excessively yin !

Never leave your clothes hanging outside overnight

For as long as I can remember, the taboo of leaving clothes out overnight has been in my consciousness. From young I had been told that hanging one's clothes out at night attracted the energies of wandering spirits to get attached to the clothes so that when worn, the bad energies of these spirits will cause us to have bad luck.

Those were of course old wives' tales. Nevertheless, feng shui masters also warn against hanging clothes and other washing on the clothesline after dark. But their reasoning has greater appeal for me. They explain this taboo in terms of the unlucky vibes caused by the clothes absorbing the excessive yin energies of the night. The same is said also for bedsheets and blankets.

It is for this same reason that feng shui practitioners of the East are often reluctant to hang clothes to dry in dark windowless rooms.

They prefer to hang clothes out in the open air and during the daylight hours. This allows clothes to absorb the *yang* energies of the bright sunlight, thereby imbuing the clothes with life energy rather than lifeless yin energy.

CHAPTER
FOUR

FENG SHUI
TO BOOST
YOUR
CAREER

ATTRACTING
POWERFUL
MENTORS

Take good care of your Northwest | TIP 109

When it comes to looking after your **success luck**, the most important part of your home, your study and your office is the Northwest sector. Not only is the Northwest the sector that most affects the luck of the family or company Patriarch, this corner also governs the quality of your mentor and patron luck.

When the Northwest of any room enjoys good feng shui balance and harmony, residents of the room will find themselves being helped along by helpful patrons. There will be many *heaven men* who will be the source of many wonderful opportunities.

When I was in my twenties, and had just discovered feng shui, just for fun I would apply every little tip I received about energizing the Northwest corner of my home and office, especially with windchimes.

I hung not one but an entire row of windchimes along the Northwest wall of my home. In my office I hung another row of windchimes and I aimed a small fan at the windchimes so that tinkling music filled my office all the time.

Needless to say, my career path was filled with countless mentors. Those days I was working with the Government, as a humble Investment promotion officer with the Malaysian Industrial Development Authority. With the help of my multiple windchimes, I enjoyed the goodwill and good regard of all my bosses, from my Division head, up to our Director General, to the Chairman and even the Minister of Trade and Industry, under whose Ministry our Authority reported to.

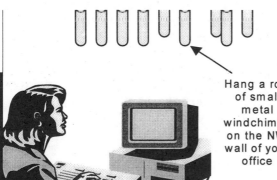

Hang a row
of small
metal
windchimes
on the NW
wall of your
office

If you feel constrained to use windchimes, another method of energizing the NW corner is to hang a picture of a large mountain to symbolize earth. Since earth produces metal, this will enhance the NW corner considerably.

CHAPTER
FOUR

FENG SHUI
TO BOOST
YOUR
CAREER

ATTRACTING
POWERFUL
MENTORS

The dragon symbol is all powerful | TIP 110

The celestial Dragon is the ultimate good luck symbol. This wonderful creature features in all the Chinese divinitive sciences, and is central to the practice of feng shui. Places with excellent feng shui are said to enjoy the dragon's precious cosmic breath. Thus placing a dragon image in the office is ALWAYS said to bring great good fortune.

The East is the place traditionally associated with the dragon ... thus placing a dragon image on the East always represents excellent feng shui. There are many ways to do this. And one can use just one of the methods or, if you are like me, you can use a combination of several methods.

Here are several different ways
to energize the good fortune breath of the dragon ...

- Purchase a dragon image and display it on a table or cabinet on the East side of your office or of your study. This can be made of ceramic, crystal, or wood. Dragons made of gold, cloisonné or other metals are not encouraged since the metal element destroys the wood element. Also, never place the dragon inside the bedroom. It is too yang a creature to symbolize inside the bedroom.

- Hang a picture of a dragon along the East wall of your office.

- Simulate the green dragon of the East in your garden by having flowering plants set in a winding flowerbed on the East Side of your garden.

- Use a table with dragons carved on the legs or a table with dragons inlaid with mother of pearl. This table can be your desk if you like but remember that not everyone has sufficient yang energy to sit at a dragon table. The same is true of a dragon chair. If you are born in the year of the dragon, chances are that sitting on furniture carved with dragon images will greatly enhance your energy levels. But be careful. As I said not everyone has the personal luck to carry this off so if after sitting on a dragon chair you fall ill, then take it that it is not for you.

- Display ceramic bowls and art objects with the dragon image. These decorative objects are deemed to be extremely fortunate. It is unlikely that such an art object is missing from the office of any successful business tycoon anywhere in the Far East.

Use the phoenix symbol

CHAPTER
FOUR

FENG SHUI
TO BOOST
YOUR
CAREER

ATTRACTING
POWERFUL
MENTORS

TIP 111

The celestial phoenix is said to symbolize the luck of wish fulfilling opportunities, and using it as a feng shui symbol is both easy and practical.

This is especially effective when activating the luck of the South corner. Look for symbols, pictures and paintings of the phoenix.

Try to get a picture of the phoenix without the dragon. To energize career luck, we do not want the dragon phoenix symbol since that symbolizes conjugal and marital happiness which is a different type of luck. We want the phoenix energy, which is *yang* on its own but becomes *yin* when placed beside the dragon.

There are beautiful modern representations of the phoenix made of crystal and embedded with gold specks that can be displayed in the South part of the office.

Alternatively you can do what I did which was to display a stunning beautifully plumed cockerel in my South corner. I had this creature displayed in a glass case all through my Hong Leong career days, and my success with this Group was amazing.

The Celestial Phoenix

The phoenix is the king of all plumed creatures, and in Chinese mythology is often represented as the mate of the celestial dragon. When placed together, the phoenix and the dragon represent a happy marriage. Thus wedding banquets are often decorated with dragon phoenix images.

On its own the phoenix symbolizes the coming of opportunities that bring success and prosperity. In feng shui the phoenix is represented by a small little mound or slightly elevated land in the South, or in the front part of the home.

If you do not have a small mound in front of your front door it is a good idea to artificially create one to represent the phoenix since this represents good feng shui. For the activating of the corners of the office– what it also referred to as the South mansion of the *8 mansions,* the symbolism of the phoenix can be contrived by using other well plumaged birds like the cockerel, the rooster, the peacock or other majestic looking bird.

CHAPTER
FOUR

FENG SHUI
TO BOOST
YOUR
CAREER

ATTRACTING
POWERFUL
MENTORS

Energizing *sheng chi* for mentor luck	TIP 112

Energizing your own *sheng chi* direction complements what you do in the Northwest corner to attract mentor luck. The latter method applies universally for everyone while the *sheng chi* direction is a personalized direction based on each individual's date of birth. It is thus different for each individual.

If you want to ensure that your working life is filled with mentors and powerful patrons, it helps to activate your *sheng chi* and the best way to do this is to enter your office each day <u>from</u> your *sheng chi* direction. This means that each morning as you enter your office, good luck follows you into the office.

Thus if your *sheng chi* is East, you should try to make sure the door into your office is facing East. Obviously this is not always possible, in which case you identify the *sheng chi* location inside your office room, and then activate that corner of your office according to the theory of five elements. Check your *sheng chi* based on your personal KUA number from Page 2, and then activate according to the element of your *sheng chi* direction using the Table below

Your KUA number	Your *sheng chi* is	What to do
1	SOUTHEAST	Place a lush plant or a water feature in your Southeast corner .
2	NORTHEAST	Use a globe, a world map or natural quartze crystal to energize the Northeast.
3	SOUTH	Install a very bright light in the South or decorate with something red.
4	NORTH	Place a water feature – a bowl with water and tortoise or a small fountain in the North.
5 male	NORTHEAST	Same as KUA number 2 shown above
5 female	SOUTHWEST	Same as KUA number 8
6	WEST	Place a large metallic object in the West.
7	NORTHWEST	Hang a windchime
8	SOUTHWEST	Place a big decorative object made of ceramic in the Southwest
9	EAST	Same as KUA 1 above

CHAPTER
FOUR

FENG SHUI
TO BOOST
YOUR
CAREER

ATTRACTING
POWERFUL
MENTORS

Activate all the symbols of protection

TIP 113

Getting ahead in one's career by catching the eye of a potential patron or mentor has a downside in that it can also simultaneously make you an unwitting victim of office politics and corporate power struggles. It is therefore always advisable to activate at least some of the symbols of protection, and strenuously observe the feng shui guidelines that guard against getting stabbed in the back. But first, let us take note of some of the symbols of protection.

Probably the best symbol of protection in feng shui is the usually benevolent white tiger that is the alter ego of the green dragon.

According to feng shui, the white tiger is always present where the dragon is deemed to be ... but he is there to protect; and so the tiger must always be *controlled* by the green dragon.

Thus the east side (the dragon) must always be higher than the west side (tiger). This is only one manifestation of the feng shui rules regarding dragon and tiger orientations.

To activate the tiger as a symbol of protection, get a ceramic tiger or any other fierce member of the wild cat family and place it OUTSIDE your office. Do not place the tiger inside your office – unless your astrological chart makes you strong enough to have a tiger in your office, it could turn its fangs on you.
Safer to place the tiger outside where it stands guard.

The head of a panther or leopard standing guard just outside your office door is also very effective as a symbol of protection. Be careful you do not put something like this inside and facing you !

OTHER SYMBOLS OF PROTECTION
In Chinese tradition, the most common symbols of protection are the pair of FU dogs commonly found outside temples and important buildings. In recent years, exquisitely made ceramic Fu dogs have been coming out of China, and you may wish to invest in a pair to place as sentinels outside your office. I place a pair outside my home, but on the wall just <u>outside</u> my main door I also place an eagle poised in the attack position as well as a wonderful painting of a lioness. All work equally well.

CHAPTER
FOUR

FENG SHUI
TO BOOST
YOUR
CAREER

ATTRACTING
POWERFUL
MENTORS

Don't get stabbed in the back

TIP 114

A great deal of good feng shui is about being defensive and watching your behind. This is to make certain you do not get stabbed in the back or are caught unawares in a difficult situation. There are specific feng shui guidelines that deal with this mainly dealing with the way you sit.

Never sit with the door behind you. If you do, you will be betrayed

DOOR

Never sit with exposed book shelves behind.

A major taboo in feng shui for the office is never to sit with the entrance door behind you. It does not matter if the door is directly behind or at a slant to your desk. You should never · sit in an orientation that makes it impossible to see who is entering your office. You should not be surprised at anytime. If this is the way you are sitting now, you will definitely get played out sooner or later, so I strongly advise that you move your desk around to face the door – even if by doing so you could well be sitting facing one of your inauspicious directions. This is how serious sitting with the door behind is.

It is also advisable never to sit with a window behind you, unless your window is facing another building that can act as a firm support for you.

Equally bad also is sitting with a bookcase behind you that has exposed open shelves. These shelves act as blades cutting into your back. Make doors for the bookcase, or move the desk around or do both.

CHAPTER
FOUR

FENG SHUI
TO BOOST
YOUR
CAREER

ATTRACTING
POWERFUL
MENTORS

Surround yourself with the *Chien* trigram | TIP 115

The trigram *Chien* is the most powerful of the eight trigrams. It represents heaven, the leader, the mentor and the patriarch. When you surround yourself with the *chien* trigram you will be surrounding yourself with precious *yang* energies since *chien* is also the ultimate *yang* trigram. This is denoted by three solid black lines, unbroken and strong, as shown in the symbol above. There are many delightful ways of achieving a roomful of *chien* energy that will help you to attract powerful helpful people into your life,

The
trigram
CHIEN

Cornices on plaster
ceilings can denote
the chien symbol

One of the prettiest and most effective method of surrounding yourself with chien energy is to have plaster cornices on the ceiling of your office. This will comprise three solid lines of plaster that not only look good and add a really nice touch to your office décor, it is also good feng shui. It is not necessary to have any other kind of pattern on the ceiling, just three lines will do the trick.

A variation of this is to place the three line cornices midway up the wall. This is also a popular interior decorative feature. I prefer to have them as cornices as I do not like cutting my walls with a decorative divider.

A third way to energize *chien* is to have a desk that has cornices carved into the desk design. Energizing the *chien* symbol on your work table is very powerful indeed.

Desks can have beautiful cornices designed into the sides to symbolize three lines.

CHAPTER
FIVE

FENG SHUI
FOR BETTER
WEALTH
LUCK

TO ENHANCE
PERSONAL
MONEY LUCK

| A SAILING SHIP LOADED WITH GOLD | TIP 116 |

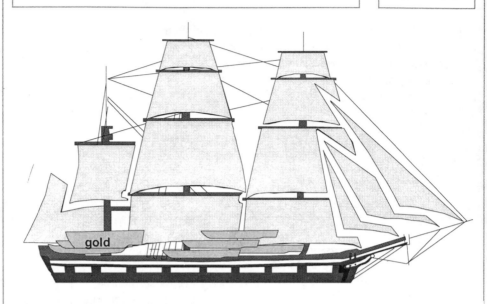

This is one of the best methods of successfully increasing your personal wealth, especially if you are a businessman. The sailing ship has always been a symbol of success in business. In the old days many old style Chinese entrepreneurs used the sailing ship as their logo since this symbolized the winds bringing more business, more trade and more turnover. Indeed, next to the dragon, the sailing ship is the most popular symbol used by Chinese businessmen.

To energize your feng shui luck for the office, place a model of a sailing ship in the vicinity of the entrance door. You must then make very certain that the sailing ship is sailing inwards, towards the inside of the office. Do not let the sailing ship face outwards, as if it is sailing away. This is vital ! Symbolically the ship must be coming IN not going away ! The same thing can be done at home. Get a sailing ship and display it near your front door.

Please note that a ship with sails to *"catch the wind* is deemed more auspicious than a model of the TITANIC, which as everyone knows sank into the Atlantic Ocean. The symbolism of the sails catching the wind and bringing gold to you is most auspicious. So if you wish to use this tip shop carefully for the right kind of sailing ship.

The next thing to do is to fill the ship with gold. Imitation gold ingots, which you can buy for a song, are easily available in the Chinese emporiums or flea markets. Stack them up inside the ship. If you cannot find these fake gold ingots, then place coins and money inside the ship

CHAPTER
FIVE

FENG SHUI
FOR BETTER
WEALTH
LUCK

TO ENHANCE
PERSONAL
MONEY LUCK

BURY A MONEY BOX in the WEST ... | TIP 117

Feng shui speaks of the great value of placing burying a Money Box in the West ... or Northwest. The symbolism that is created is most auspicious for the entire household, especially if there is also a small mound to represent a mountain. This symbolizes a mountain of gold in one's backyard. Since earth produces gold in the cycle of elements, this method of energizing feng shui is deemed to be doubly auspicious.

The money box can correspond to the strong box or safe of modern times. If you have a safe. It is a good idea to place it in the West or Northwest – both of which corners represent the metal element.

 Remember that the Chinese character for metal, shown here on the left is also the character for gold, which in turn represents wealth. The Northwest is also the place of the family Patriarch, so energizing the Northwest is excellent feng shui for the entire family.

 Place your safe in the West or Northwest. And if you have a garden, bury a money box, preferably filled with coins in the west part of your garden as shown in the sketch below. You can use leftover change to fill up your money box, but proper coins are better than pennies. Chinese coins with the yin yang characters and the square hole in the center are best.

This mound of earth can be artificially created for the west or Northwest of the garden.

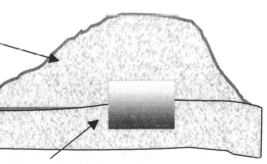

A metal money box filled with coins buried under a mound of earth is very auspicious. Make sure the money box is placed inside a plastic container as you don't want it to rust.

CHAPTER
FIVE

FENG SHUI
FOR BETTER
WEALTH
LUCK

TO ENHANCE
PERSONAL
MONEY LUCK

PUT FENG SHUI COINS IN YOUR PURSE | TIP 118

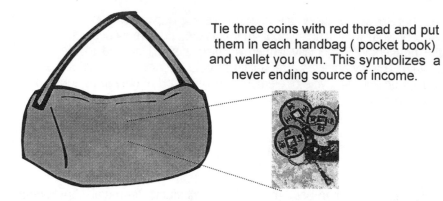

Tie three coins with red thread and put them in each handbag (pocket book) and wallet you own. This symbolizes a never ending source of income.

One of the best tip I ever received concerned all the small little ways I could use three Chinese coins to activate and symbolize a never ending source of income for myself. The easiest and most novel recommendation I put into practice was the placement of three coins tied with red thread into my wallet. I found it so effective that I started placing coins in ALL my purses and wallets and handbags. In the interest of fashion, I change my hand bag frequently to match my clothes; so to make certain I was never short of cash I put these feng shui coins in ALL my purses. I might add that it is not necessary to put more than 3 coins. In fact 3 is a very good symbolic number which represents the union of heaven, earth and man – itself an auspicious combination. Never use 4 or 5 coins since these are not regarded as lucky numbers. You may if you wish use 6,7 or 8 coins – all of these are lucky numbers.

I have recommended this tip to many people and one of my favourite little gifts is to give a red packet with three coins tied with red thread to symbolize the offering wealth luck to my friends. This is a very auspicious habit to cultivate since the act of giving is in itself most auspicious, especially when giving something as symbolically auspicious as three coins in a red packet. Do this when you attend auspicious occasions. Add them to the presents and gifts you give to celebrate the weddings and birthdays of your loved ones and good friends. They are very auspicious indeed.

Remember that it is the red thread that activates the *yang* energies of the coins and that by themselves, these coins do not have feng shui significance. If you do not have red thread, you may use a bright red ribbon. It has the same effect although the Chinese find it even more auspicious when the coins have been expertly tied into never ending auspicious knots.

CHAPTER
FIVE

FENG SHUI
FOR BETTER
WEALTH
LUCK

TO ENHANCE
PERSONAL
MONEY LUCK

AT WORK SIT FACING YOUR SHENG CHI | TIP 119

DRAW AN ARROW
ON YOUR DESK
TO REMIND YOU !

The most potent method of enhancing your wealth luck is to use compass formula feng shui, particularly the Pa Kua Lo Shu formula of feng shui which reveals your *sheng chi* or most auspicious direction, based on your date of birth. To find out your personal *sheng chi*, first calculate out your KUA number, using the formula below, and having done that refer to the Table on the right to identify your *sheng chi* direction. Then always SIT facing this direction.

CALCULATING YOUR KUA
NUMBER (adjust for lunar calendar)
Add the last two digits of your date of birth, and keep adding until you get a single number. Then:
For men: deduct from 10 and the answer is your KUA number.
For women: add 5 and the number is your KUA number.

If the answer is a double-digit number, add the two digits until it becomes a one-digit number.

YOUR KUA	YOUR *SHENG CHI* DIRECTION	YOUR OTHER GOOD DIRECTIONS
1	SE	N,S,E
2	NE	W,SW,NW
3	S	N,E,SE
4	N	S,E,SE
5	NE/SW*	W,NW
6	W	NW,NE,SW
7	NW	W,NE,SW
8	SW	NW,W,NE
9	E	SE,N,S

Men with KUA number 5 the sheng chi is NE while women with KUA number 5 the *sheng chi* is SW. The best tip I can give you is to always remember your good directions.

CHAPTER
FIVE

FENG SHUI
FOR BETTER
WEALTH
LUCK

TO ENHANCE
PERSONAL
MONEY LUCK

CREATE A PERSONAL WEALTH VASE | TIP 120

This is a very personalized tip passed to me by a practicing feng shui master from Taiwan. It was during my corporate career days in Hong Kong. He told me that he often advised his rich clients to each create a personal wealth vase to preserve their wealth.

Get a beautiful and valuable vase, he advised. A vase made of the earth or metal elements would be acceptable. Earth element vases would be porcelain or crystal while metal element vases would be made of either copper, brass, silver or gold. Needless to say the more expensive the material, the more auspicious would be the vase created. Thus a gold vase would be infinitely more auspicious than a silver one, which in turn would be more auspicious than copper or brass. It was also acceptable to have silver gold plated vases since a solid gold vase would be much too expensive.

Fill your wealth vase with precious gems. If you can afford it, fill your vase with diamonds. If you cannot then fill your vase with semi precious stones – crystals, quartzes, amethysts, citrines, tigers eye, lapis, malachite, pearls, and so forth. Put your jewelry inside your wealth vase.

I personally used a crystal vase, filled with semi precious stones to make my wealth vase, and because this was of the earth element I placed it in the earth element corner of a cupboard in my bedroom ie the Southwest. Corner. The Northeast is also acceptable. For those who opt for metallic vases, place them in the West or Northwest corners.

Please note that the personal wealth vase should be kept hidden away, inside a cupboard in your bedroom. The wealth vase must never face the front door since this symbolizes it draining away. Never show anyone your wealth vase.

CHAPTER
FIVE

FENG SHUI
FOR BETTER
WEALTH
LUCK

TO ENHANCE
PERSONAL
MONEY LUCK

KEEP A PET TORTOISE AT HOME

TIP 121

The tortoise is such an excellent energizer, you should also have it in the home.

HOW TO KEEP
YOUR PET TORTOISE

Use a decorative ceramic or porcelain pot that is at least 18 inches in diameter. Keep it half filled with water and place a small rock in the center. This allows your tortoise the choice of being in or out of the water. Remember that tortoises are reptiles. Change the water three times a week and always let tap water stand for a while for the chlorine to evaporate. Feed with fish food or fresh green vegetables.

It is possible to attract good fortune and luck into the home by keeping pet terrapins. These beautiful domesticated mini tortoises can be purchased from Fish shops, and they make excellent pets for young children. When the children grow up, these tortoises usually lie forgotten in their little ponds. Nevertheless, because they are such hardy reptiles they live on, growing slowly and not requiring very much care.

Tortoises bring great good fortune and protection to households that keep them. In old China, many of the Imperial palaces and homes of the wealthy mandarins had tortoise ponds. In Malaysia, tortoise ponds can be seen in the Kek Lok Si temple in Penang Hill, and also in Genting Highlands.

On an individual level, anyone can tap into the luck of the tortoise. DO not forget that this humble reptile is regarded as a very auspicious celestial creature who is believed to be imbued with strong protective powers. For this reason, I keep a pet terrapin and he lives in a large ceramic pot in the NORTH part of my home.

It is not necessary to keep more than one, since ONE is the number of the north location, and the tortoise in feng shui is associated with the north, a single tortoise represents excellent feng shui. Do not worry that the tortoise will feel lonely. This is a creature who is a natural loner who happiest when he is alone. If the tortoise you keep dies, simply get another one. This simply means your pet has successfully protected you from a minor disaster.

CHAPTER
FIVE

FENG SHUI
FOR BETTER
WEALTH
LUCK

TO ENHANCE
PERSONAL
MONEY LUCK

DESIGN AN AUSPICIOUS CALLING CARD | TIP 122

KONSEP LAGENDA
231 lorong Bukit Pulaui
Kuala lumpur
Malaysia
Lillian Too
Executive Chairman

Use feng shui dimensions and make at least one side of the card less than 5.1 cms. Anything from this to 16.5 cms is deemed inauspicious. Thus my own calling card shown here on the left is less than 5.1 cms in both width and length.

Be very careful when designing your corporate logo. Never go for any design that is sharp, pointed or angular, and especially if one of the points is inadvertently pointed directly at your company name. I strenuously warned a bank that had just such a logo. My advice was ignored and that bank is one of the casualties of the Asian economic crisis and now no longer exists.

Also be very careful about shapes. Rounded, curved shapes are always to be preferred over angular or triangular shapes.

If you have no choice in the matter of your company logo, then I strongly advice you to make certain that none of the angles are pointed directly at your name on the card. Move it out of the "firing range".

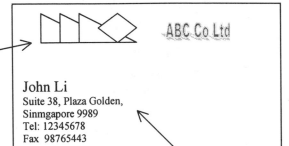

ABC Co Ltd

John Li
Suite 38, Plaza Golden,
Sinmgapore 9989
Tel: 12345678
Fax 98765443

When positioning your name and address, do make certain that the result is a well balanced card. Here the words and text are all on one side of the card making the card unbalanced.

FENG SHUI GUIDELINES
ON COLOURS
IN CALLING CARD DESIGN

Black printed on white is better than black printed on beige. So white calling cards are to be preferred to off whites.

When using two colors make certain the colors are harmonious. Good color combinations are black with green, black with brown, black with blue, and black with metallic.

Inauspicious combinations are black with red, black with orange, and black with yellow.

CHAPTER
FIVE

FENG SHUI
FOR BETTER
WEALTH
LUCK

TO ENHANCE
PERSONAL
MONEY LUCK

CREATE A PERSONAL WATER DRAGON | TIP 123

The ancient classical texts on water dragons is so important in feng shui it would take an entire book to comprehensively explain the many variations of successfully building a water dragon.

The feng shui dragon is a most auspicious creature, and creating a water dragon in the home is one of the best ways of energizing wealth luck

However, it is possible to create a personal water dragon, using plants and the presence of flowing water. A mini fountain is the most suitable for creating a water dragon in the living room. Get a small gold dragon and place it in a fountain, allowing the water to flow over the dragon.

You should identify the exact spot in your living room, where placing this water fountain will bring you the best kind of luck.

Based on the calculations of *fey sin* or *flying star*, for this period of 7 ie. from now until the year 2003, water fountains are best placed in either North, East, Southeast, or Southwest. These are the only four locations that are auspicious during this period of 7. The BEST place for your water fountain depends on the exact direction your main door faces. Use the table here to determine your BEST location.

Direction which the main door faces	Bearing exact degrees	BEST LOCATION for water fountain
SOUTH 1	157.5-172.5	NORTH
SOUTH 2/3	172.5-187.5	NORTH
NORTH 1	337.5-352.5	NORTH
NORTH 2/3	352.5-007.5	NORTH
EAST 1	067.5-082.5	EAST
EAST 2/3	082.5-097.5	EAST
WEST 1	247.5-262.5	EAST
WEST 2/3	262.5-277.5	SOUTHWEST
S.WEST 1	202.5-217.5	NORTH
S.WEST 2/3	217.5-232.5	SOUTHEAST
S.EAST 1	112.5-127.5	SOUTHEAST
S.EAST 2/3	127.5-142.5	SOUTHWEST
N.EAST 1	022.5-037.5	EAST
N.EAST 2/3	037.5-052.5	SOUTHWEST
N.WEST 1	292.5-307.5	NORTH
N.WEST 2/3	307.5-322.5	SOUTHEAST

CHAPTER
FIVE

FENG SHUI
FOR BETTER
WEALTH
LUCK

TO ENHANCE
PERSONAL
MONEY LUCK

Invite the God of Wealth into your home | TIP 124

The Chinese have several Deities they regard as the Wealth God. Probably the most popular is the God of Wealth featured on the left. This is the God of Wealth I have *"invited"* into my home, and which I have recommended with huge success to many friends of mine.

His name is *Tsai Shen yeh* and he is often depicted, as shown, sitting on a Tiger, to symbolize his control over this animal. In the lunar years of the Tiger, displaying this wealth God is said to particularly auspicious.

I do <u>not</u> worship or pray to this Deity. Instead I treat his presence in my home as purely symbolic. For good measure, I also hang a specially knotted cluster of nine Chinese coins, tied with red thread to activate the prosperity attributes of the coins.

The best place to locate the God of Wealth is on a table or side board that is between 30 to 33 inches high directly facing the front door. Thus the first thing you see upon coming into the home is the Wealth God. He greets the *chi* coming into the home, transforming it into healthy prosperous energy that then flows through the rest of the house. If this particular location is already taken up by the family altar, then place the God of Wealth in the corner of the living room that is diagonally opposite to the main entrance door. The God of Wealth should face the front door. This is shown in the sketches below. Please do not place your God of Wealth in your bedroom or dining room. The living room is the best place. Only the three star gods, the *Fuk Luk Sau* can be placed in the

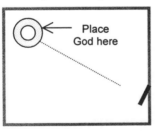

dining room. Another deity usually regarded as bringing wealth is *Kuan Kung,* who is equally popular with the Chinese.

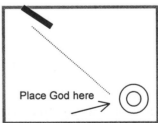

CHAPTER
FIVE

FENG SHUI
FOR BETTER
WEALTH
LUCK

TO ENHANCE
PERSONAL
MONEY LUCK

A THREE LEGGED FROG FOR LUCK | TIP 125

Frogs and Toads are generally regarded as auspicious creatures to have around the garden, and the Chinese believe that if there is a whole family living in your backyard, it means you will be protected from any dangers or bad luck which might be coming your way.

It is the three legged frog however that is supposed to be extremely auspicious, and it is easy to find these good fortune symbols in any Chinese supermarket.
The three legged frog is usually depicted as having three coins in its mouth to signify he is bringing gold into your home. This same symbolism can also mean taking gold out of the house. So the way the frog is placed becomes important.

Place the three legged frog symbol near the vicinity of the front door BUT facing inwards, as if it has just come into the house. Do not allow the frog to be placed directly facing the door. This symbolizes gold going OUT of the house.

The best place is to place the frog at the far corner diagonally opposite the main door. Put it under a table, inside a cupboard or hidden away under chairs and other furniture.

Frog symbols should not be placed in the kitchen or any of the bathrooms and toilets. In these inauspicious places the frog turns malevolent and instead of bringing good fortune, they tend to attract bad luck chi that cause havoc with the energy of the home.

It is also not a good idea to put them in the bedrooms. They are best when placed in either the living or dining areas of the home, and remember; Never facing out, always facing in !

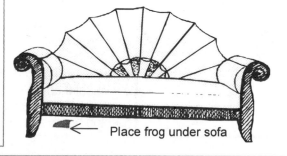
← Place frog under sofa

CHAPTER
FIVE

FENG SHUI
FOR BETTER
WEALTH
LUCK

TIPS FOR
RETAIL
SHOPS

Make better turnover with tinkling bells | TIP 126

Place tinkling bells high above the door outside the shop

Chinese shopkeepers have always known about the efficacy of tinkling bells to attract customers into their shops. These little metal bells create *good chi* each time someone opens the door to come into the shop, in the process bringing in the luck required to enhance the shop's turnover. This method is especially effective for shops selling personal items and products like jewelry shops, men's and ladies boutiques and accessories shops.

The tinkling bells can be made of any kind of metal and to increase the effectiveness of the bells, tie a red ribbon to activate its intrinsic yang energy. The ideal number of bells should be 6 or 7 although most shopkeepers usually keep only one pair of bells. There are two methods of attaching these bells onto the doors.

1. they can be attached to either door handles on the outside of the shop or
2. they can be attached high above the door in such a way that each time the door opens the bells will sound.

Place a bunch of 6 tinkling bells directly opposite the door here to entice in the good *sheng chi*

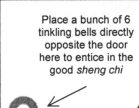

INSIDE THE SHOP
Tiny tinkling bells can also be placed inside the shop, anywhere along the west or northwest wall OR directly facing the entrance door, high on the ceiling. This serves to entice the good *sheng chi* to enter into the shop. These bells need not be seen. Their presence in the shop is symbolic, and after you have placed them there you can forget about them. In olden days, bells usually symbolized the announcement of good news and hence were symbols of good fortune.

CHAPTER
FIVE

FENG SHUI
FOR BETTER
WEALTH
LUCK

TIPS FOR
RETAIL
SHOPS

Stick three coins on your cash box | TIP 127

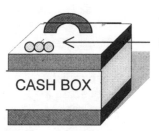

Stick three coins on top of your cash box, like this ...

CASH BOX

Tie three Chinese coins in a straight line, with the yang side facing upwards, and then tape them with transparent cellophane tape onto your cash box to increase your daily take from cash sales.

Old Chinese antique coins, particularly those from the Chien Lung period of the Ching dynasty has many different uses in the practice of feng shui. If you cannot get hold of the antique variety, imitation Chinese coins can also be used for all your feng shui enhancements that are related to increasing your wealth and income luck. But whatever coins you do use, always make sure that you wash them with sea salt before you start to use them. This gets rid of any negative energy that may be still clinging onto the coins. This is merely a precaution and you should not fret if you have already started using these coins and did not clear them of negative energies this way. Those of you who have used the coins provided in my feng shui kit need not worry since these coins are not antique. They are imitation Chinese coins and thus do not have any negative energies attached to them.

TWO ADDITIONAL WAYS OF INCREASING
TURNOVER LUCK WITH THREE CHINESE COINS

Stick the three coins on your cash register.
This is a very effective way of generating better sales for your retail shop and it also has the advantage of making anyone who has just bought something, to buy an additional something else. In other words it multiplies the amount of purchases made by customers who enter into your shop. Place the coins on the inside of the cash register so that it is not so obvious. There is no need to advertise your use of feng shui.

Stick the three coins on top of your Invoice book
The sales or Invoice book is another business tool that can be effectively enlivened with the use of Chinese coins. Simply tape three coins tied with red string onto the cover of your sales book, making sure that the yang side of the coins are face up. The yang side of the coins is the side with four sides. The other side – the yin side is not for energizing this way. Use transparent cellophane tape to do this as we want the coins to be seen. Be like me, and do the same thing on all your important files.

CHAPTER
FIVE

FENG SHUI
FOR BETTER
WEALTH
LUCK

TIPS FOR
RETAIL
SHOPS

Install a wall mirror to reflect the till | TIP 128

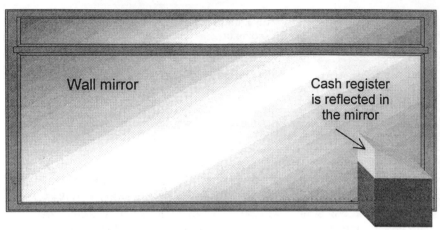

Wall mirror

Cash register
is reflected in
the mirror

As well as good fortune antique coins, Chinese shopkeepers are also fervent believers of placing large wall mirrors inside their shops. This not only doubles the products on display, thereby signifying the prosperity of a well-stocked shop. The mirrors also create massive doses of yang energy because it doubles all activity within the shop. Mirrors do wonderful things for business income when it reflects the cash register. This literally symbolizes a doubling of turnover. Do not use a tiny little hand held mirror, like a friend of mine when I passed on this tip to her. I recall her telling me she did not believe in feng shui because she said my tip did not work. And then, quite by chance I went to her shop and saw her pathetic little mirror! It was no wander the mirror did not work. What it was reflecting was not the cash register but the door! So all the good fortune chi entering her dress shop was going right out again! I made her install a wall mirror in the correct way (see sketch below) and since then she has had no complaints.

An excellent use of mirrors in retail shops is to have them on all the walls except those that directly reflect the entrance door. Mirrors are shown as dotted lines here.

INSIDE THE SHOP
The use of mirrors is an excellent way of magnifying all the good energy of your business. If you have pillars, wrap them with mirrors, and if you have display cabinets, also wrap them with mirrors. And if possible, place mirrors on all the walls around the shop except those directly opposite the entrance. This way all the products displayed will be reflected in the mirror. Also all customers will similarly be reflected in the wall mirror. This doubles the good fortune.

CHAPTER
FIVE

FENG SHUI
FOR BETTER
WEALTH
LUCK

TIPS FOR
RETAIL
SHOPS

Hang bamboo inside the entrance

TIP 129

The hollow stem of the bamboo plant has many different feng shui applications and one of the easiest method of activating the long term good fortune of the bamboo is to hang a pair of bamboo stems above the entrance of the shop. This is shown in the sketch on the right where the bamboo stems are placed tilted towards each other to simulate the *pa kua* shape. The bamboo stems are also tied with red ribbon to energize them.

It is not necessary to place too many of these bamboo stems in your shop. One pair is good enough and if you find it difficult to place them above the entrance door, another good location is on the wall opposite directly facing the entrance door. These stems need not be too large not too fat. A small six inch piece will be good enough but make certain that both ends are open.

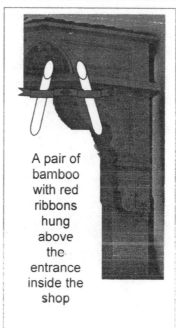

A pair of bamboo with red ribbons hung above the entrance inside the shop

THE BAMBOO PLANT
Is one of the most popular and potent symbols of longevity. It represents strength in circumstances of adversity and the ability to go through all kinds of stormy weather. Used as a feng shui tool they do not just symbolize long life and good health. The bamboo is also a very powerful sign of good fortune. It is always good feng shui to have a painting of the bamboo in the house or office. When you hang the bamboo stem in your shop it creates excellent protective and good fortune chi inside your shop. Your business will survive hard times and flourish in good times.

CHAPTER
FIVE

FENG SHUI
FOR BETTER
WEALTH
LUCK

TIPS FOR
RETAIL
SHOPS

Three tips for shop layout design | TIP 130

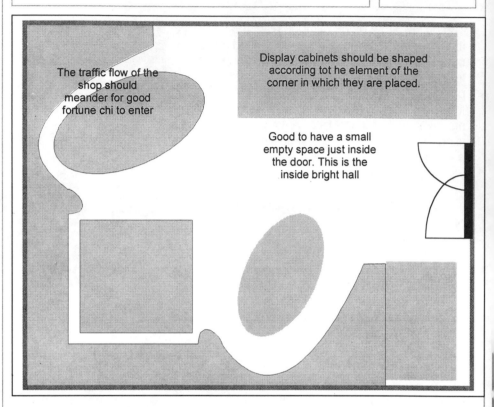

The traffic flow of the shop should meander for good fortune chi to enter

Display cabinets should be shaped according tot he element of the corner in which they are placed.

Good to have a small empty space just inside the door. This is the inside bright hall

When you are designing the layout of your shop be mindful of these three important feng shui tips. You can be as creative as you wish, and you can use any kind of color scheme that pleases you but observing these three tips will bring your shop excellent feng shui.

Firstly: you should let your shop door open into a small empty space where there are no cabinets, screens or furniture to block the chi entering your shop.

Secondly you should select shapes for your display cabinets according to the corners where they are placed, making sure that you do not position any cabinet or table with the sharp edge pointed at the entrance door.

Thirdly, if you want customers to actually buy your products once you have succeeded in enticing them in, you must design a traffic flow within the shop that meanders rather than move in straight lines. A meandering traffic is simply excellent for business. Go to any Marks and Spencer shop and you will see what I mean by having a meandering flow of traffic.

CHAPTER
FIVE

FENG SHUI
FOR BETTER
WEALTH
LUCK

TIPS FOR
RETAIL
SHOPS

Design or display the horse shoe shape | TIP 131

I find it really interesting that the horse shoe is regarded as a good luck symbol in the West. In feng shui the shape of the horse shoe very eloquently describes the ideal land configuration. It is a perfect representation of the green dragon white tiger configuration that defines feng shui. Thus hanging a horseshoe is also considered favourably by feng shui.

The horse shoe shape however is regarded as particularly auspicious when used as display cabinets in retail shops, or when incorporated into wall designs. Simply hanging a specially designed wall cabinet that has been fashioned into the horseshoe shape is considered very lucky indeed. However it is also important that you place the shape correctly. Do not let it directly face the door entrance, and definitely do not place the rectangular part of the shape directly facing the door.

LUCKY SHAPES FOR DISPLAY CABINETS

Regular shapes like the rectangle and the square are excellent. Just make sure the sharp edges are never pointed to the door or to the cash register.

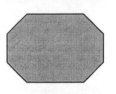

The Pa Kua shape is also very auspicious. It is excellent for displaying small items of high value like jewelry, accessories, and other designer items. The Pa Kua shape can be elongated without losing its essence.

Circular shapes are also auspicious. They can be round or oval. These shapes do not have sharp edges and they are well balanced.

131

CHAPTER
FIVE

FENG SHUI
FOR BETTER
WEALTH
LUCK

TIPS FOR
RETAIL
SHOPS

Good feng shui design for restaurants | TIP 132

Traditional Chinese restaurants are the best places to go to if you want to see feng shui motifs being incorporated into restaurant design. The dominant colour used will always be red because the restaurant business is deemed to belong to the *fire* element. There will also be excellent lighting and round pillars will usually have colourful carved dragons and phoenixes. These Chinese restaurants of another time are getting scarce these days as the *modern* look takes over. Thus I have now seen restaurants that use, not the *fire* element in their décor but rather the *water* motif. Quite rightly, those who have opted for the water rather than the fire motif for their restaurant business seem to be doing extremely well, and especially their dinner sittings. This is because such restaurants have liquor licenses and this part of their business seem to do extremely well when the water motif is energized.

Incorporating a water motif or pattern (shown here) in restaurant business seems to bring tremendously good business, and especially in giving a huge boost to the wines and spirits part of the business.

This antique robe is most unsuitable as restaurant décor – business will suffer.

This word 'fook' brings good fortune

CHAPTER
FIVE

FENG SHUI
FOR BETTER
WEALTH
LUCK

TIPS FOR
RETAIL
SHOPS

Fire symbols for real estate business | TIP 133

Good feng shui for those in the real estate business requires the fire symbol. This is because in the productive cycle of relationships the fire element produces earth. And earth symbolizes real estate.

Fire symbols usually imply that the office/shop should:

- Be well lighted especially the foyer area and the area that is in the vicinity of the entrance door.
- Have something red. This can be one wall or a door painted red. Or it can be red curtains or a red carpet, or even a painting that is predominantly this color.
- The incorporation of the sun symbol shown below ....

If you are in the real estate or property business feng shui should be of particular importance to you since you will have to advice customers on how the feng shui of any property can be improved. I am so often asked to give my opinion on pieces of property by my friends, and I try to tell them that most properties in the city have what I term very average feng shui – usually not very good, but also not bad. I have always advised that it is what you do with the property and how you decorate it which makes it good or bad for you.

There is of course also the directions and orientations to take account of. Depending on your personal good luck directions some houses will obviously represent better luck for you than other houses.

Having said that, there are buildings and houses where the feng shui is seriously afflicted by the proximity of lethal poison arrows. The particularly difficult ones to counter are structures like transmission towers, a huge wall, a flyover, an elevated road, a water tank, a massive building or an oncoming road – these types of man made structures are all found in the city and their negative energy are really very tough to overcome or diffuse. As a real estate broker you should be wary about recommending or taking on such properties.

CHAPTER
FIVE

FENG SHUI
FOR BETTER
WEALTH
LUCK

TIPS FOR
RETAIL
SHOPS

A plant in the East ensures growth

TIP 134

Place a plant like this in the EAST of your shop OR at the entrance to ensure continuous growth of your business.

Chinese shopkeepers and business people in Hong Kong, Singapore and Malaysia always displays a pair of these lime plants dripping with fruits during the new year.

CHAPTER
FIVE

FENG SHUI
FOR BETTER
WEALTH
LUCK

TIPS FOR
RETAIL
SHOPS

Balance the elements of your business | TIP 135

If yours is a jewelry business try to make all your display cabinets curve, as shown here. This is because the gemstones and jewelry business belong to the metal element and will thus benefit hugely from the curved shape. Let traffic move in a curved fashion inside your shop, and avoid red in your décor. This is because fire destroys metal and is NOT good for this business. Earth energies, on the other hand will benefit you so do place objects made of clay and crystals.

If you are in the antique business, selling Buddhas and other decorative items collected from exotic places, you should be careful when handling deities and religious artifacts. Buddhas for instance, and statues of ethnic Gods should always be treated with respect. Remember that these are holy objects, which carry a great deal of symbolic energy. So do place them on tables- elevated at least higher than people moving around the shop. The sleeping Buddha for instance should never be placed on the ground. Nothing brings greater misfortune than disrespect shown to holy objects. So if you are in this business do be careful. Also, since you are dealing with antiques which give off a lot of yin energy, it does help if you create some yang energy in your shop. Keep the shop well lighted. Let there be music in your shop, and even paint one of the walls a yang color.

If yours is a souvenir shop selling curios and other decorative objects made of wood, like the exquisite swan shown here, you might want to activate the wood energies of your shop. Bring in a nice bushy plant. It can be fake but it should look fresh and vigorous. This will enhance your turnover tremendously. Place a bright light just outside your entrance to create yang energy.

CHAPTER
FIVE

FENG SHUI
FOR BETTER
WEALTH
LUCK

TIPS FOR
RETAIL
SHOPS

Earth energy brings good fortune | TIP 136

If you want your business to benefit from earth energy, you should energize the three earth corners of your shop.

These three corners are:

1. the center
2. The southwest corner and
3. The northeast corner. Place ceramics, pottery and crystals in these corners either as decorative ornaments featured here or as furniture.

Earth energy is strongest in the Southwest – the place of the trigram KUN. Place a small collection of pottery in this corner and shine a bright light to activate its energies. It is more effective if the light is red in color since this strengthens the fire element which produces earth.

Mother of pearl furniture are excellent energizers for the wood corner. Chinese furniture seldom use nails, which are deemed to be bad luck when, used on furniture.

This belief can be traced to the five elements and their destructive cycle. Metal is said to destroy wood, and in the old days, emperors and rich mandarins alike would not sit on chairs nor sleep on beds that had nails driven into them.

CHAPTER
FIVE

FENG SHUI
FOR BETTER
WEALTH
LUCK

TIPS FOR
TYCOONS
WITH
CORPORATE
BUILDINGS

Guard your corporate signboard | TIP 137

PLAZA TARA GLOBAL

The corporate signage is one of the most important things which any successful business must protect against bad feng shui. Together with the main door, these represent the two things most vulnerable to negative energies that may be present in the surrounding environment. The first golden rule is to make sure that the signboard carrying your corporate name should be placed high up on your corporate building, as shown here. The corporate name should not be placed on the ground level. It will cause the eventual demise of the company

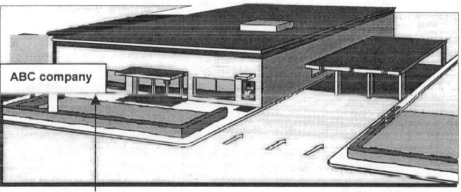

ABC company

A signboard placed on the ground, as shown above has negative long term feng shui consequences. In an economic downturn such companies will be amongst the first to find themselves in financial difficulties. Always place the signboard at the highest part of the building. This will safeguard you against being pulled down by the tough times of an economic recession.

THINGS THAT CAN HURT YOUR CORPORATE SIGNBOARD

Even when your signboard is placed high on your building, the following are some structures you need to watch out for.

- Elevated highways & flyovers
- Transmission and other towers
- Neighboring buildings
- Elevated city railways
- Sharp edges of buildings

CHAPTER
FIVE

FENG SHUI
FOR BETTER
WEALTH
LUCK

TIPS FOR
TYCOONS
WITH
CORPORATE
BUILDINGS

LUCKY NUMBERS BRING PROSPERITY | TIP 138

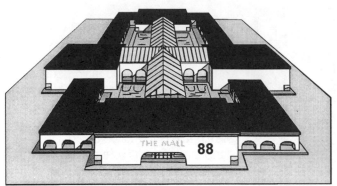

If you are fortunate enough to have an auspicious number in your building's address, display the lucky number prominently to bring in all that good fortune !

In new York, all the buildings have their numbers prominently displayed on the front of the building. It is perhaps a requirement and works really well for all those buildings with auspicious numbers while working against those with *death* numbers,

AUSPICIOUS NUMBERS
Are numbers that end with all the lucky numbers which are:
1; 6, 7 ,8 and 9
All these five numbers are very lucky numbers, but the number 8 seems to be the most popular simply because it sounds like *phat* which means prosperous growth in Chinese. The number 9 is regarded as the premier number by most feng shui masters because it signifies the fullness of heaven and earth. The number 9 never changes no matter how many times it is multiplied by itself. 9 times anything leads to 9 .. thus 9X 3=27 and 2+7=9 and so forth ..
you can test this out yourself and see the power of 9.
The numbers 1, 6 and 8 together , in any order, is regarded as a most splendid combination representing enormous good luck, while the number 7 is lucky because it is the number that represents this period. It will cease being a lucky number by the year 2003, after which 8 becomes the number of the next period i.e. between 2004 to 2023 It is for this reason that 8 is regarded with such favour – because it represents both current and future prosperity.

UNLUCKY NUMBERS
The number 4 is extremely unpopular because it is considered the death number simply because it sounds like 'die". For many people however the number 4 has brought tremendous good luck ! In feng shui the numbers 2 and 3 together is considered a hugely bad combination leading to misunderstandings that lead to severe problems. But worse than that is the dreaded 5. When the 5 appears in feng shui it brings huge problems.

CHAPTER
FIVE

FENG SHUI
FOR BETTER
WEALTH
LUCK

TIPS FOR
TYCOONS
WITH
CORPORATE
BUILDINGS

AUSPICIOUS CORPORATE LOGOS | TIP 139

The corporate logo should always be designed with an eye to its feng shui significance. There are some general guidelines that are useful to follow, and if you have your own business, you might want to pass on these criteria to your art director or advertising agency.

- Circular and curved designs are safer than designs that have sharp edges and angles. Thus triangles and zig zags are not advisable. Please note that companies that have an angular graphic as a logo that do well ALWAYS have their angles pointed outwards AND NEVER AT THEIR CORPORATE NAME. The HongKong Bank's logo is an excellent example of a pointed logo that works in favour of the company.

- The use of animals in corporate logos usually signifies courage, strength and resilience. The Dragon is the ultimate auspicious logo and most companies that use the dragon usually go from strength to strength. The two companies I worked with had excellent dragon logos. I designed both logos, making the Hong Leong Dragon fat and pregnant to symbolize the Group's ambitions of becoming a global conglomerate giving birth to many subsidiaries. That was over fifteen years ago and the Group is today a most successful global corporate player. I also designed the logo of Dragon Seed my department store- here I w anted a happy dragon suggestive of quality. In both cases I made the dragon poised for flight upwards – suggestive of soaring ambitions. Other animal logos would be the tiger and the lion but neither will ever be able to match the dragon in auspiciousness.

- The use of abstract designs and shapes – squares circles and other five, six or eight sided shapes – require careful thought. These can create or have extremely bad negative connotations resulting in bad feng shui.

- The use of flowers is excellent but can never be as powerful a symbol as a living creature. A bud about to open is more auspicious than a fully opened flower, in the same way that suggestions of spring colors (green) is always more auspicious than the colors of autumn (oranges and browns.) One denotes a business about to take off while the other describes a business about to die. In the same way sunrises are to be preferred to sunsets.

Buds about to open would be more auspicious than a flower in full bloom. Left is better than right.

CHAPTER
FIVE

FENG SHUI
FOR BETTER
WEALTH
LUCK

TIPS FOR
TYCOONS
WITH
CORPORATE
BUILDINGS

Grand Entrances for excellent feng shui | TIP 140

The grander your corporate building, the grander should be the main entrance door. Otherwise there will be no balance. Residents of large buildings that have small doors cannot have big luck. There is insufficient to go around. The good energy cannot enter the building in sufficient quantities.

A grand entrance is one that looks imposing and firm. It should preferably be properly decorated with guardian lions, high columns or other equally solid looking or protective feature. Having said this, do not over do things. It is also important to understand that when the main door is too big, the building becomes overwhelmed with too much energy. This is often more dangerous than an insufficiently big door

FU DOGS or other guardians

228 Eighth Avenue

The above is a very typical entrance of large apartment blocks in New York. In feng shui terms this door is considered sufficiently *"grand"* for this building. It is solid, double sided and has a canopy covering the entrance. This resembles a small foyer type area outside the door and is a good feature to have. If the door of this building were directly facing Central Park residents will enjoy excellent feng shui.

It is a very good idea to install a pair of symbolic protective creatures. Many successful businesses in the Far East have guardian Fu dogs placed on guard outside the entrance of their buildings. The Hongkong Bank has its famous pair of giant lions – these British lions were fashioned as replicas of the lions in Trafalgar Square in London but they have successfully the fortunes of Hong Kong Bank since its founding in the previous century.

CHAPTER
FIVE

FENG SHUI
FOR BETTER
WEALTH
LUCK

TIPS FOR
TYCOONS
WITH
CORPORATE
BUILDINGS

Beware of inauspicious shapes | TIP 141

The Sphinx is too yin an idea to be successfully used as a theme for a modern shopping mall.

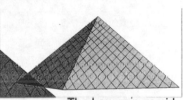

The Louvre pyramid has good feng shui.

The Sydney Opera House

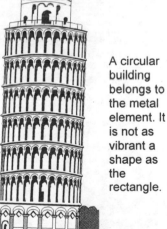

A circular building belongs to the metal element. It is not as vibrant a shape as the rectangle.

Tycoons who have the resources to build large buildings – corporate headquarters, hotels and shopping malls – are usually too busy to bother about feng shui. Thus, large developments with serious feng shui mistakes do get built –usually, with serious consequences for the companies that built them.

In Malaysia we have a shopping mall with an entrance fashioned to resemble a lion. It was meant to be the Sphinx but later became lion. I am sure the owners should not be too surprised that no one likes shopping inside the belly of a lion !

I have also seen the pyramid shape become increasingly popular. These shapes have tremendous impact on the surrounding environment. They emit energies that are not suitable for a living environment. The pyramid (and the Sphinx) are reminiscent of tombs, and tombs are very very <u>yin</u> places. Pyramid roofed buildings that house corporate head offices can cause the eventual demise of these companies. One pyramid that is excellent feng shui however is the Louvre museum. It is lucky because of the way it was built – it is made of glass and it lets in masses of sunlight. Also, museums benefit hugely from yin energy.

The Sydney Opera House has shapes that suggest the fire element. It is therefore a very yang building, and is a lucky building, but being built by the sea pits fire with water. The good fortune is thus tempered by the element imbalance. The leaning tower here is round – suggestive of metal. Round buildings are not as good as rectangular buildings.

CHAPTER
FIVE

FENG SHUI
FOR BETTER
WEALTH
LUCK

TIPS FOR
TYCOONS
WITH
CORPORATE
BUILDINGS

Head offices must have foundations — TIP 142

One very severe feng shui affliction has to do with the presence of empty space in some of the modern high rises that are being built.

These "*holes*" cause the *chi* to flow <u>away</u> rather than <u>towards</u> the building. If your corporate head office is built with the ground level exposed in this way, and as shown here, all and any good fortune coming your way simply flows away again.

Such buildings are described as lacking in foundation. The affliction becomes even more severe if the Board rooms and offices for the top brass of the company i.e. the directors, are located in that part of the building that has nothing but empty space below (arrowed in the sketch)

Buildings like this also lack a proper entrance door, which signifies *no mouth for the good luck to enter.* If your building has this feature, I strongly suggest building walls and making use of your ground floor level.

Otherwise this emptiness on which the rest of the building stands will cause offices located above to either close down, move away or simply go bust.

Empty space below. Occupants above this space will suffer from lack of foundation

Spaces on ground level are also bad

CHAPTER
FIVE

FENG SHUI
FOR BETTER
WEALTH
LUCK

TIPS FOR
TYCOONS
WITH
CORPORATE
BUILDINGS

Watch the back and the front	TIP 143

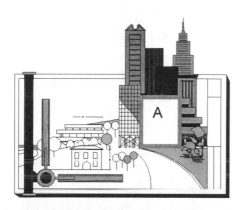

This building here (shown in white and marked A) enjoys excellent feng shui. Taller and larger buildings behind offer protection, as do the higher buildings on the left and right. And then in front is the empty field and curved road. The empty field symbolizes the auspicious bright hall, while the road symbolizes the wealth-bringing river

MAIN POINTS TO NOTE

** Every building must observe the general guidelines of good feng shui which advises that the building behind you is slightly higher than yours and the buildings by the left and right should not be higher than the buildings behind. This creates the green dragon white tiger configuration that describes classically excellent feng shui. When designing and planning your corporate head office you might want to take these rules on landscape feng shui into account. Even if you do nothing else this would strengthen your feng shui.

** In front of you there should be empty land. This is one of the most auspicious feature, and if you are able to tap its good effect is even better than having a view of water. If there is a patch of empty space in front of your building, then I very strongly suggest that you enlarge your main door to welcome in all that marvelous good *sheng chi* accumulating there. Use a glass door (as opposed to a solid door) so that the *chi* can come right in ! This does not mean you may not have a solid door further inside the building. But it is excellent to keep the door apparently open to capture the *chi*. In Singapore there is a brand new building which faces the small empty space of a bank building, and there are three massive planters in front of its main entrance that resemble "*offerings*". This is a wonderful sign of auspicious good fortune, since it appears like the bank is making the offerings. This is excellent for business.

** Every high rise building must have a proper main entrance and a proper back door. Buildings that have too many doors and entrances, to an extent that it is not possible to identify the main entrance suffer from fluctuating fortunes that will finally cause it even to collapse. Symbolically this means that the company it houses will have no sense of direction. There will be frequent changes of ownership and management.

CHAPTER
FIVE

FENG SHUI
FOR BETTER
WEALTH
LUCK

TIPS FOR
TYCOONS
WITH
CORPORATE
BUILDINGS

Never ever redevelop your building | TIP 144

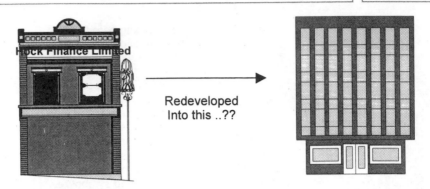

Redeveloped
Into this ..??

I was in Singapore on a business trip in March this year and had tea with a new friend I had met recently while we were both on pilgrimage in India. Derek is the son of a family business, which owned one of Singapore's small but successful banks. Unfortunately the horrible financial and economic crisis which hit South East Asia, and especially Indonesia late last year has taken its toll of companies in all the countries of the region. Derek's family bank was one of those hit because of lending exposures to Indonesian businessmen. When we spoke that afternoon, merger talks were already being finalized that would in effect put his family bank out of existence.

I had witnessed Derek's great generosity and kind heart at first hand and felt genuinely sad at what was befalling his family. But Derek's sense of humour was wonderful ... *"that's why lah ... you should know what ... they say if you redevelop your building and pull down your signboard you will collapse. So we redeveloped our building and see .. not even finished redeveloping ... and the bank is already gone!"*

Indeed Derek is right. This is a cardinal rule of business feng shui. No matter how much you want to take advantage of advances in the construction industry and no matter how much the land on which the original building stands, has gone up in value, your head office building should be sacrosanct. Pull down the building that saw your family business flourish and you could well be signing the death warrant of your business.

So do resist the temptation of higher plot ratios and greater financial gains ... respect the good feng shui of the old building which brought so much wealth. Clean it up and renovate with modern facades by all means **but** do not pull it down. By damaging the foundation of your corporate headquarters, you will damage your entire business as well.

CHAPTER
SIX

FENG SHUI
FOR
DIFFERENT
ROOMS IN
THE HOME

TIPS FOR THE
FRONT PART
OF YOUR
HOME

A bright hall brings great good fortune | TIP 145

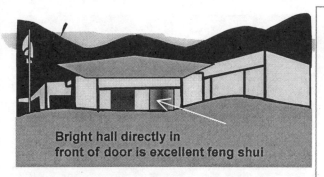

Bright hall directly in front of door is excellent feng shui

The *bright hall* of feng shui is a super important feature to try to arrange for your home. It is for this reason that whenever my friends ask my advice on how they should go about choosing which unit to purchase when confronted with say 200 units to choose from, I always advise them to select house that face a playing field. With empty land in front of you, there is NO way you will not become prosperous. And if you are lucky enough to have a landed house with a garden you MUST make sure that you orientate your door to open out into the garden. Then keep that part of the garden empty of trees and too many plants. Small low level shrubs are fine but not plants that grow too tall

The house sketched here on the left has excellent landscape feng shui. The hills behind on its left and right create natural arm chair formations while directly in front of the main door is a beautiful empty piece of land. This garden is the bright hall of feng shui, a feature so auspicious, rich businessmen of Singapore and Hong Kong often purchase the neighbours land simply to create this bright hall.

WHY DOES TMC MINI MARKET HAVE SUCH GOOD BUSINESS ?

In my part of town in Kuala Lumpur Malaysia, we have a supermarket that is doing so well and making so much money, it has become the talk of the area ...

Apart from excellent service and good prices **TMC mini market** also has excellent feng shui. It has a door so wide (about 25 feet) that directly faces an empty piece of land (the bright hall), it appears as if the whole supermarket opens onto the bright hall. If you are greedy and want to really capture the good *chi* of your bright hall, then make your front door BIG. When the door is big more of the prosperity *chi* will flow into your home. Then make sure the door opens for at least a part of the day ...a closed door cannot admit *chi* into the home.

In the case of TMC, not only do they have BIG doors – they have also placed ALL their <u>cash registers</u> directly facing their bright hall ! They will therefore continue to flourish and prosper as long as the piece of land across the road from their front door stays unbuilt.

CHAPTER
SIX

FENG SHUI
FOR
DIFFERENT
ROOMS IN
THE HOME

TIPS FOR THE
FRONT PART
OF YOUR
HOME

Winding pathways to slow down the *chi* | TIP 146

There is both sunlight and shade in this garden and a winding pathway
in a garden complements the excellent balance between yin and yang energies.

Use decorative stepping stones to create a winding pathway in your garden. This provides the linkages from one part of the garden to the next. No matter how small your garden is, these pathways always slow down the *dragon's chi*, thereby making it auspicious.

I use round concrete slabs to simulate coins, but any shape and any kind of pathway will do the job. If you want you can place a series of stepping stones that resemble Chinese coins that ends in the vicinity of your main door.

Your pathway can thus be made of pebbles, stones, wood or even tar ... just make certain it is curved and not in a straight line. If you do have a straight path, and you do not want to make any changes, then you must make sure the straight pathway does not stop directly in front of a door, A straight pathway has the potential to become a poison arrow.

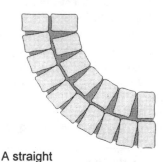

A straight pathway becomes a poison arrow in the garden and if it is pointed at or ends at the door, it spells bad luck. A curved pathway is much better.

CHAPTER
SIX

FENG SHUI
FOR
DIFFERENT
ROOMS IN
THE HOME

TIPS FOR THE
FRONT PART
OF YOUR
HOME

Plants to attract precious yang energy | TIP 147

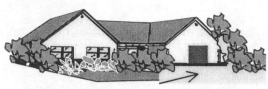

Plants enhance the yang growth energy created by the bright hall in front of the main door.

Gardens play a crucial role in enhancing your good feng shui. Having a garden around you, however small it is attracts precious yang energy to surround your home. The presence of healthy green and growing plants. attract the vital energy that bring auspicious luck.

A home filled with vibrant growing plants. immediately suggests the presence of the dragon's cosmic breath. In the old days one method feng shui Masters used to locate the auspicious dragon's lair was by looking at the lushness of greenery along hillsides. It was where grass grew strong, vibrant and lush that represented the place where the green dragon resided. Such those places were deemed to enjoy an abundance of the cosmic breath, the good *sheng chi.*

Thus one way of simulating this is to look after the plants in your garden. Making certain they are lush and healthy.

MISSING CORNERS
If you have missing corners in your house layout, you can use plants to symbolically create usage of the empty space. The sketch above shows a house that has a U shape, with the empty space being in the center. Note that plants have been used to regularize the empty space.

GUIDELINES ON PLANTS IN THE GARDEN
Healthy growing plants are always a good idea. Having said that however here are some feng shui guidelines concerning plants.

- Try to leave the space directly in front of your main front door empty of plants. Here, it is far more auspicious to try and achieve the effect of the *bright hall*.
- Trim your plants at least once every three weeks. Overgrown plants that send branches willy nilly is bad feng shui.
- Get rid of all dried leaves and faded blooms. Anything dead creates yin energy that create negative feng shui energy.
- Be careful of plants with thorns being too near the vicinity of your front door. Such plants create protective energies that are welcome, but they should not be too near the door.
- Always make certain that the East and Southeast of your garden is covered with lush greenery and blooms. Healthy plants in this part of the garden bring you wealth luck.

CHAPTER
SIX

FENG SHUI
FOR
DIFFERENT
ROOMS IN
THE HOME

TIPS
FOR THE
FRONT PART
OF YOUR
HOME

Let flower beds embrace the home

TIP 148

This garden also has sunlight and shade at the same time thereby creating excellent balance of yin and yang energies. Note how the flowerbeds embrace the garden.

GUIDE TO AUSPICIOUS COLORS OF FLOWERS

Use element analysis to design the color scheme of flowers. Determine the compass directions of your garden and then follow the chart below.

Compass sector of your garden	Auspicious colors of flowers
North	Blue, purple,
South	Reds. and yellows – all shades
East	Blues and purples
West	White
SEast	Same as East
SWest	Same as South
NEast	Same as South
NWest	Same as West

It is a very good idea to have flowering plants in the front part of your garden. This is particularly auspicious when the front part of your garden is facing South, or one of the South directions i.e. Southeast and Southwest. And for the front part of your home, allow any shade of red to dominate. Thus you can have flowers in any shade of red, from the light pinks of carnations and fuschias to the deep dark reds of peonies, bouganvillea and roses.

CHAPTER
SIX

FENG SHUI
FOR
DIFFERENT
ROOMS IN
THE HOME

TIPS FOR THE
FRONT PART
OF YOUR
HOME

Beware arrows that hit the door

TIP 149

The driveway of this home is especially auspicious, the water feature facing the front door is excellent. *Potential* poison arrows are the pillars and the road, but both have been arranged harmoniously resulting in good feng shui.

In this example, the curved drive way is very correct and auspicious BUT the tree from across the main door has grown so large, it has become a poison arrow. Far better to chop down this tree.

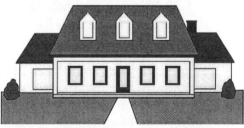

The straight pathway leading up to the main door is a poison arrow. It may look harmless, but the killing energy of such a driveway can sometimes be very severe.

POISON ARROWS

These are structures and features in the surrounding environment that causes bad feng shui that result in severe ill fortune and bad luck.

Effective feng shui practice requires the ability to spot the secret poison arrows of one's environment. It takes some experience to identify these harmful structures because many of these structures appear very innocent and quite harmless. Thus something as natural as a road can be a poison arrow if it approaches your home, and especially your main front door as a long and straight road.

The more obvious poison arrows that may be hitting your main door in the outside environment are:
1. a straight road.
2. A triangular roof line
3. A high wall nearby
4. A transmission tower
5. A telephone pole
6. A tree trunk
7. A tall straight building
8. Edge of two walls.

149

CHAPTER
SIX

FENG SHUI
FOR
DIFFERENT
ROOMS IN
THE HOME

TIPS
FOR THE
FRONT PART
OF YOUR
HOME

A door flanked by water spell tears | TIP 150

Water flanking the door is bad feng shui

I once visited the mansion of a very powerful and popular Minister who was also a very good friend of mine. I was immediately taken aback by the large "moat" the Minister had surrounding the mansion. To enter the house visitors had to cross a bridge that was placed over the moat. Inside the moat were stunning Japanese carp and beautiful water lilies. Despite these lucky features, the water was wrong. I did not have the heart to tell my friend that water on both sides of the front door means tears. I did not want to offer unsolicited advice.

Thinking back I should have, because my poor friend has since suffered defeat in an important election, had to put up with infidelity, and has since suffered rather unfortunate and humiliating events.

In your eagerness to introduce a water feature into your home, please note these three points:

1. That you get the positioning of your water feature correct. I have written an entire book on water feng shui, and in all my talks I strenuously warn against the introduction of water into your garden or home without first checking things out. Next,

2. That you should never over do the presence of water since too much water can spell extreme bad luck, especially when also placed incorrectly. It is for this reason that I always frown on swimming pools in private homes. They are simply too large a mass of water to take lightly. Pools are great in clubs and condominiums but can be dangerous in private residences where the land area is too small. Such pools could well drown you !

3. That you do not place water on both sides of your main door. This spells tears i.e. severe loss - a sudden fall from power and, sometimes even death.

CHAPTER
SIX

FENG SHUI
FOR
DIFFERENT
PARTS OF
YOUR HOME

TIPS FOR THE
FRONT PART
OF YOUR
HOME

Gate design and Fu dogs | TIP 151

FU DOG

AUSPICIOUS GATE DESIGN

FU DOGS

For protection against every kind of bad luck, traditional Chinese homes are seldom without a pair of FU DOGS. There are no rules on what size these Fu dogs should be, but they should balance and reflect the size of the home they are supposed to be guarding! In the picture above you can see one of a pair of Fu dogs that I place high up on either side of my gate.

Fu DOGS should ideally be placed high up as shown. They can also be placed at table level but they should not be on the floor. Always put them on a stand of some kind. FU DOGS are easy to find in Chinese pottery and ceramic shops. Both Taiwan and China in recent years export exquisitely authentic copies of traditional FU DOGS. Mine are made of ceramic and are two feet high.

GATE DESIGN

Your gate should be at least 70% solid and ideally should not have holes in them. I made those holes in my gate as a compromise – i.e. to see who is at the gate when I get visitors and also for purpose of allowing the breeze through. But feng shui prefers completely solid gates.

Secondly it is very auspicious to design a gate which has the center higher than the sides, as shown. This symbolize that one will attain all of one's goals. If your gate has the center lower than the sides, it signifies failure in your career.

Please note that your gate is NOT your main front door. But it is the entrance into your home. Thus although the direction and feng shui of your main door is more important than your gate, it is nevertheless advisable to also make certain that your gate is not hit by secret poison arrows.

CHAPTER
SIX

FENG SHUI
FOR
DIFFERENT
ROOMS IN
THE HOME

TIPS
FOR THE
FRONT
PART OF
YOUR HOME

A spacious foyer brings good feng shui | TIP 152

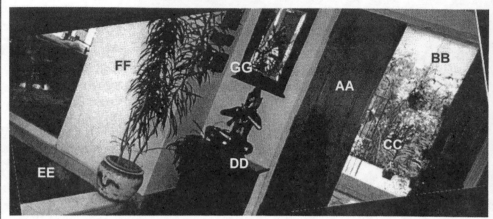

The foyer of my home (above) has several features with feng shui significance that are worth noting.

AA There are two panels to the door The open door is the larger of the two. This is an auspicious feature.

BB. Unfortunately the door faces a wall about twenty feet away. Ordinarily this is not good so I have placed hanging plants between the wall and the door.

CC I make sure the hanging plants – mainly orchids are flowering all the time. As soon as the flowers fade I change them. This creates good energy for the tiny bright hall which I have also constructed here.

DD This Thai musical Buddha is the patron of wealth and good income. The Thais believe that having him in the foyer attracts in the good *chi.*

EE My koi pond is on the left hand side of the door. If the pond were on the right, my husband will develop a roving eye !

FF This plant covers the sharp corner edge

GG The mirror does NOT reflect the main door and was put there to "extend" the wall outwards because of the small missing corner here.

Note
This is the door which I constructed for my husband. It opens out, and faces his best direction according to the Compass School feng shui formula.

In my house we have two front doors – one each for me and my husband. This was necessary because we have different *sheng chi* directions. What is great for me is deadly for him and vice versa. We therefore enter and leave the house through different doors. Over the years I discovered that by doing this to overcome the problem of us having different good and bad directions has benefited us enormously.

CHAPTER
SIX

FENG SHUI
FOR
DIFFERENT
ROOMS IN
THE HOME

TIPS FOR THE
FRONT PART
OF YOUR
HOME

Let your altar face the door directly

TIP 153

I really do not know about other religions but to us Chinese, we believe that the most auspicious place to locate the family altar is that part of the hall that directly faces the front door so that the minute we walk into our homes we see the altar. In accordance with feng shui I also recommend that the altar be placed on the Northwest part of the house or room since the NW represents heaven.

However irrespective of where you place your altar, please observe that you should always place your Buddha or Kuan Yin deity on an elevated place.

The altar should also be clean at all times. Joss sticks and incense should never be allowed to appear uncared for. This is especially important if the altar is placed directly facing the front door.

Keeping the altar lights turned on at all times attracts in the good *chi* energy. It is even more powerful than having a crystal chandelier. In my home I have activated both – altar lights and a chandelier !

Basic guidelines on altar placement

Those of you who have altars might want to take note of the following guidelines.

- The deity or holy object (whether statue or painting) should not share a wall with a toilet. It is most inauspicious.
- The deity or holy object should not be directly below a toilet upstairs. This too is most inauspicious.
- The deity should not be placed directly facing the door into the toilet. This direction is most inauspicious.
- The deity should not be sitting directly underneath an exposed overhead beam.
- The deity should not be directly facing a staircase. It is most inauspicious.
- The deity should not be underneath a staircase since this means that residents will regularly step over the deity. This is most inauspicious.
- The deity should not be placed in any bedroom where the resident is having sex regularly. This is very inauspicious.
- The deity should always be placed indoors or with a roof over its head. Deities placed outdoors should have special altars made for them.

153

CHAPTER
SIX

FENG SHUI
FOR
DIFFERENT
ROOMS OF
THE HOME

'IPS FOR THE
FRONT PART
OF YOUR
HOME

Make your front door auspicious   TIP 154

My fishpond
The picture on the left here is the fishpond which is located on the left hand side of BOTH of my doors (My husband and I each have our own doors because we belong to different compass direction groups). We have had this pond for over twenty years so some of our Japanese carp (koi) are as old as the pond. We have over a hundred carp inside the pond and we replenish them each year because old carp do die off. When any of your fish die on you there is no need to worry. Just replenish with news ones.

I also have a tortoise pond in the North, at the back of my house. The North is the best place to keep tortoises since this is the direction that signifies the celestial tortoise.

In addition to protecting the front door from being hurt by external poison arrows, it is also important that the space around it be properly designed by incorporating auspicious feng shui features.

The best feature to have near the vicinity of the front door is a water feature which can be a miniature fountain, an artificial waterfall or a fish pond like the one shown above. With this kind of water feature you can add fresh plants and flowers, and you can make the water flowing so that fresh *yang* energy is being created continuously through the day.

Build the water feature on the left side of the door (**inside looking out**) and fill the pond with carp, goldfish, the arrowana or tortoises. Do not mix fish with tortoises. Decide which you prefer and keep only one species.

It is vital that the water filter is kept turned on twenty fours throughout the day and night so that the water is always clean and flowing. Feed your fish with high protein food which also contains vitamins. This makes their scales glow with good fortune.

CHAPTER
SIX

FENG SHUI
FOR
DIFFERENT
ROOMS OF
THE HOME

TIPS FOR
HOUSE
LAYOUTS

Front doors should not face a toilet

TIP 155

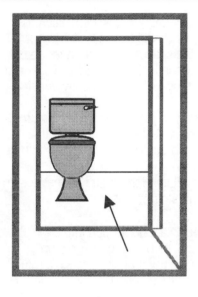

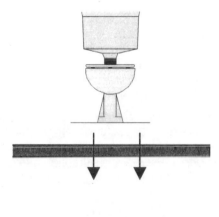

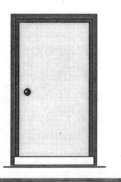

TOILETS

Cause real havoc when they are located near the vicinity of the front door. When you are planning the layout of your home,

Try to avoid having the guest toilet located directly in front of the door (as shown). If your toilet can be seen from the front door, you should endeavour to change the toilet door, entering it from another wall. If there is sufficient space place a solid divider (a curtain is not solid enough) to separate the toilet door from the front door.

Toilets above the main door

This is another arrangement that creates extreme bad luck. The negative energy from the toilet on the floor above permeates the ceiling and flows downward, causing severe affliction to the door and bringing extreme bad luck to residents

If you have this problem, you should try to either change the location of the toilet, or change the location of the main door, and when doing layout planning you should definitely ensure that your main door is clear of any toilets upstairs.

If you have this problem and you are unable to move either the door or the toilet, then the only thing you can do is to shine a very bright light upwards at the ceiling in symbolic attempt to push the bad *chi* away from the main door. This can only be partially successful but it is better than doing nothing.

CHAPTER
SIX

FENG SHUI
FOR
DIFFERENT
ROOMS IN
THE HOME

TIPS FOR THE
FRONT PART
OF YOUR
HOME

The taboos of the main door
TIP 156

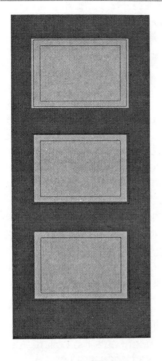

The feng shui of the main door is the single most important feature to get right. This is the *kou* or mouth of your living space. It is through the main door that all your good luck comes to you. It is also the place where good luck can so easily transform into bad luck.

It is not enough only to place auspicious features near the main door. In fact more important than that, you must watch out for all the things that must not be near the main door. We have already dealt with the taboo of toilets. Here are additional design layouts concerning the main door.

- Do not let your main door open into a cramped space. If your foyer is too small, either not have a foyer at all, or place a mirror on a wall of the foyer that does not reflect the door directly. The bright hall works on both sides of the door.
- Do not let the main door open onto a long straight corridor. This is like having a poison arrow pointed at your back each day as you leave the home and hitting at your heart when you return. Place a screen like the one shown here to block the killing energy.
- The screen is also very useful when your main door is in a straight line with two other doors. This *three doors in a row* configuration makes the energy rush through, transforming it into killing energy.
 Placing a screen between the doors is a good solution to this problem.

The main door should always open into a large and spacious room – the living room is ideal for this purpose.

- If it opens into the <u>dining room</u>, residents think only of eating.
- If it opens into the vicinity of <u>the kitchen</u> all the luck of the family could get washed away. There will also be rivalry and a lot of anger in the household.
- If it opens too near <u>a bedroom</u> residents become indolent and lazy.

CHAPTER
SIX

FENG SHUI
FOR
DIFFERENT
ROOMS IN
THE HOME

TIPS FOR
HOUSE
LAYOUTS

Deal with pillars facing the main door | TIP 157

USING PLANTS

This square pillar faces my main door directly and its sharp edge creates an average size poison arrow that hits at the good luck entering my home.

To cope with this small problem, I am making use of a very beautiful and lush plant, whose leaves effectively dissolve the effect of the sharp edge simply by covering the edge.

In the wall behind which is also visible from the door, I have hung a copy of a painting of three beauties playing the flute. This is an excellent way of enticing in the wonderful *sheng chi*. You can use any kind of plant to camouflage any pillars or sharp corners that may be hurting your day but the leaves must be lush and green. A fake plant is acceptable.

As for the painting, you too can use any kind of painting, poster or print of a musician. Welcoming the luck in with music is a very Asian tradition which has its roots in feng shui.

CHAPTER
SIX

FENG SHUI
FOR
DIFFERENT
ROOMS IN
THE HOME

TIPS FOR THE
FRONT PART
OF YOUR
HOME

Make your staircase lucky & auspicious | TIP 158

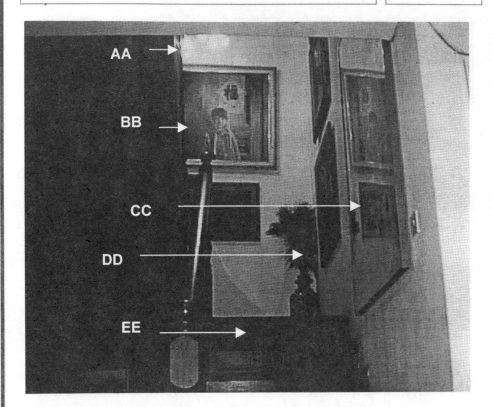

The staircase is often neglected by feng shui practitioners, and this is such a pity because there are so many wonderful ways of enhancing the feng shui of the staircase, so that you encourage good fortune to rise and make its way to the private quarters of the family. The picture above offers some tips.

- **AA:** Always keep the staircase and the landing well lighted since this attracts the chi to flow up the stairs.
- **BB:** Hang a lucky auspicious painting at the landing. Mine has the word *fook* which means *great good luck* on it.
- **CC:** If your staircase is narrow, one way to overcome it is to hang a large mirror to visually widen it. This will allow for greater good fortune.

- **DD:** I place a pot of peacock feathers here as further enticement for the good luck to come upstairs.
- **EE:** My staircase steps are solid. There are no holes between the steps. This ensures that any money in the family does not seep out. If your staircase has holes between the steps, you should immediately close them with additional pieces of wood.

Double the luck of your dining room

TIP 159

CHAPTER
SIX

FENG SHUI
FOR
DIFFERENT
ROOMS IN
THE HOME

TIPS FOR
HOUSE
LAYOUTS

The family dining room can be made to be extremely auspicious if one wall of the room is completely covered with a wall mirror. This is shown in the picture above. This is the dining table where my small family eat together when we are not entertaining friends to dinner. It is small so each time we eat it appears that our table is simply overflowing with food –an excellent representation. The mirror then proceeds to double the wealth of food on the table.

Next I have made the shape of this family table round. The Chinese love round dining tables because this shape represents metal, which is another word for gold, or money. Round is also representative of the luck from heaven. Having said this I might add that square tables and rectangular tables are equally lucky.

It is also an excellent idea if the dining room has a wall or door that opens into a small courtyard. This will attract good fortune into a place where the family gather together everyday. Plant auspicious flowering and fruiting plants in the courtyard. The orange or lime plants would be ideal.

CHAPTER
SIX

FENG SHUI
FOR
DIFFERENT
ROOMS IN
THE HOME

TIPS FOR THE
FRONT PART
OF YOUR
HOME

Choose kitchen locations carefully | TIP 160

When you are planning the placement and orientation of your kitchen, it is useful to understand that kitchens are not places where good luck can be created. Kitchens, however, are excellent for pressing down on bad luck. Thus if for any particular year a certain direction has bad luck under the flying star school then having the kitchen there located there will keep the bad luck under control. Similarly if any direction represents bad luck for you according to the KUA formula, then a kitchen located there kills off your bad luck.

From a feng shui perspective the kitchen is thus important for being a useful method of countering bad luck in your living space.

Additional notes on the kitchen can be summarized as follows:
- Always locate the kitchen in the inner half of the home.
- Never let the kitchen be too near the front door.
- As you enter the home, kitchens are better placed on the left than on the right hand side of the home. This keeps the *white tiger* under control.
- It is better not to have the back door located in the kitchen.
- Do not put mirrors or mirror tiles in the kitchen. These can cause severe misfortune to befall the family.

THE OVEN & COOKER
This should never be placed in the NORTHWEST part of the kitchen. This creates the vastly unlucky situation of having a fire at heaven's gate. The outcome of this arrangement is either that your house will burn to the ground OR you will suffer severe financial loss. Please try to observe this guideline as the bad luck incurred is severe.

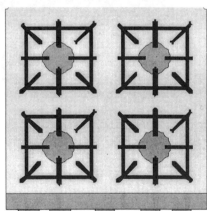

Also bear in mind that the stove should not be next to the sink, the refrigerator or the washing machine since this will create a clash between the fire and water elements. This clash of elements causes quarrels and misunderstandings in the family. The situation is made worse if the stove and the water structure or appliance are directly opposite each other since this will be the confrontational mode.

Finally kitchens should have at least one window. Windowless kitchens are both impractical and also bad feng shui.

CHAPTER
SIX

FENG SHUI
FOR
DIFFERENT
ROOMS IN
THE HOME

TIPS FOR
HOUSE
LAYOUTS

Dining room feng shui

TIP 161

FUK LUK SAU
These Gods of Health, Wealth and Longevity are a most important addition to dining room décor. The Fuk Luk Sau on the left here are made of cloisonné. I place them on a high side table in my family dining room to assure my family of the good fortune of always having something to eat, and being healthy enough to eat the good food available to us. Fuk Luk Sau (in ceramics, ivory and metal) can be bought at any Chinese supermarket.

- The dining room should always be on a higher or equal level as the living room. If you have a multi level house. Make certain you and your family eat on the higher level. As an aside, I might add here that houses that have too many split levels that result in half floors and mezzanine floors usually suffer severe bad luck during astrologically bad times. The bad luck affects the family patriarch most. If there are many different levels in your home, make sure the family eats at the higher level. And definitely you should have the bedrooms in the top floors.

- If you have more than one dining room in the home, make sure that the one where the family eats regularly is the higher of the two.

- The dining room should not be next to the bedroom. This creates a great deal of unsettling *chi* to both rooms.

- If there is a toilet located on one wall of the dining room, please keep the toilet door closed at all times. In fact it is very unlucky to have a toilet located too near the dining table.

- Hang pictures of food and flowers in the dining room if you want a touch of art but strenuously avoid pictures of animals, birds or other animals.

- Do not let the dining room be located at the end of a corridor. It creates enormous bad luck for the family to eat in such an unlucky room.

CHAPTER
SIX

FENG SHUI
FOR
DIFFERENT
ROOMS IN
THE HOME

TIPS FOR THE
FRONT PART
OF YOUR
HOME

Living rooms must have one solid wall | TIP 162

There should be at least ONE solid wall in any living room, and this wall should preferably be directly facing the door into the room. This allows the *chi* to flow into, and around the room, instead of escaping through windows that may have been placed directly opposite the door.

When arranging the layout of your halls and living rooms, be sensitive to the flow of traffic as you move from one room to the next. Try to allow for a meandering flow because this causes the chi to be beneficial. One way of doing this is the place connecting doors diagonal to each other.

AS you can see, my way of doing this is to have very large and very wide archways connecting one hall to the next. This not only gives me a feeling of spaciousness (which is always excellent), it also enables me to use plants and furniture to create the meandering flow of energy that I want to achieve. It is not always necessary to have to many walls in the home. Large archways always give a better energy flow than many small rooms.

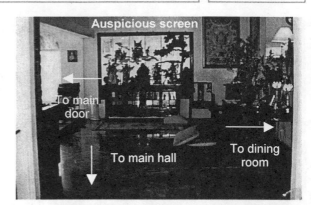

Auspicious screen — To main door — To main hall — To dining room

In my hall, shown above, three sides are open and only one wall is solid. There are no windows because each of the other three sides open into other rooms. Such a layout allows this hall to double up as the internal bright hall. Allowing space for the chi to settle and accumulate before moving into the rest of the house.

In the main hall shown below, there is also only one solid wall, on which are placed good fortune and auspicious paintings as well as the family portrait that creates the feng shui for us to stay happily together. The feng shui of family portraits has already been dealt with elsewhere in this book. The best place to hang such portraits is pride of place in the main hall.

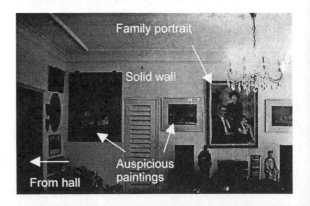

Family portrait — Solid wall — Auspicious paintings — From hall

CHAPTER
SIX

FENG SHUI
FOR
DIFFERENT
ROOMS IN
THE HOME

TIPS FOR
HOUSE
LAYOUTS

Windows, beams and corners ...   TIP 163

The ratio of windows to doors should not exceed three windows to one door. If you exceed this ratio, more luck is flowing out than coming in ... the picture here shows the living room of my home in Kuala Lumpur. You will see solid walls balance nicely with the windows of my living room.

In the second living room shown in the picture below, the ratio of windows to doors is maintained. Please note that all windows have been built very low to the ground.

This helps to bring the garden into the home and this creates additional *yang* energy.

CORNERS AND BEAMS

I have always told my friends that it is impossible to get everything correct in feng shui. In my house for instance I have quite a number of protruding corners and exposed overhead beams. Examples of this are shown in the pictures above, top and bottom respectively. These imperfect feng shui structures are due to continuous addition and renovation to the house. As our incomes improved our home has become bigger and bigger but these additions often caused unsightly structural beams to become exposed as walls got knocked to enlarge the rooms.

THE CURES

For the exposed beam shown in the picture on top I use windchime to dissolve the killing energy emanating from the beam. I also make sure that the table is placed away from under the beam so that no one sits directly below the beam.

For the corner you can see that I have used a very high foliage plant which covers the edge of the wall very effectively. In fact every corner edge and every pillar in my home will have a plant in front. These plants usually last for only 6 months after which they usually succumb to the poison arrow of the edge. They wilt and die off and have to be replaced. Hence sometimes I use fake plants.

CHAPTER
SIX

FENG SHUI
FOR
DIFFERENT
ROOMS OF
THE HOME

TIPS FOR THE
FRONT PART
OF YOUR
HOME

Take care of your bedroom feng shui | TIP 164

GUIDELINES ON BEDROOM FENG SHUI.

- Place all sleeping quarters in the higher levels of the house.
- Do not have the doors of bedrooms directly confronting each other. This creates confrontations between residents of the rooms.
- Do not have odd shapes for bedrooms. L shaped rooms caused by attached bathrooms are not auspicious. Squares and rectangles are the best.
- Do not have a bedroom that forces you to place the bed between the door and the toilet door.
- Place the bed diagonally opposite the door.
- Do not sleep with your head or your feet directly pointed at the bedroom door.
- The bedroom door should not directly face a staircase, a toilet or anything sharp, like the edge of opposite walls.
- Do not place the bed directly under an exposed overhead beam.
- Do not place the bed under a window.

Keep curtains drawn when you sleep

Sleeping with a window directly above the bed creates unbalanced sleep and is generally not advisable. However, it is sometimes difficult to get one's feng shui perfect in every respect. I have to place my bed this way because I wanted to tap my best direction. Placing the bed anywhere else in the room also had me sleeping under an overhead beam. So I chose this arrangement as, on balance being the best feng shui solution.

The result ?

I benefit from the good luck of sleeping with my head pointed to my best direction, but I suffer from the occasional attack of insomnia because of the unbalanced energy.
Most times I keep the curtains drawn in order to close out the window. This helps to alleviate the problem of the window to some extent.

Thus, you simply cannot get everything perfect according to feng shui. No one can get their feng shui a hundred percent correct. Getting a feng shui consultant in will not help. It is better for you to understand all the options facing you, understand the different feng shui methods and techniques you can apply, and then choose from various alternatives. The formulas on directions and locations are excellent but if you cannot tap them in your present room, then choose another way of enhancing your feng shui.

CHAPTER
SIX

FENG SHUI
FOR
DIFFERENT
ROOMS IN
THE HOME

TIPS FOR
HOUSE
LAYOUTS

Secondary doors are also important

TIP 165

This secondary door in a neighbour's house is located in the North part of the house and this supports her main door which is facing East .. water produces wood in the cycle of elements.

Note the tortoise pond in a container ...

Also note the plants which create good growth energy for the door.

One of the most effective ways of enhancing the feng shui of your home is to have a secondary door that is either orientated or located in the part of the house whose ruling element supports or produces the element of the main door.

Example:
If your main door is facing South and this is an auspicious direction and location for you, then having a secondary door in the East or Southeast will magnify the luck of the whole house. This is because the element of the East and Southeast is *wood,* and *wood* produces the *fire* element of the south. The elements are thus in harmony.

If Main door is located or facing this direction: ↓ ▼	Secondary door placed here will benefit ↓ ▼
SOUTH	East and Southeast
NORTH	West and Northwest
EAST or SOUTHEAST	North
WEST or NORTHWEST	Southwest or Northeast
SOUTHWEST NORTHEAST	South

CHAPTER
SIX

FENG SHUI
FOR
DIFFERENT
ROOMS IN
THE HOME

TIPS FOR
HOUSE
ELEVATIONS

The importance of having a proper roof | TIP 166

A flat roof creates the impression that something is missing

With a proper roof over the home, shelter is assured.

A cardinal rule of feng shui relates to the concept of shelter. For your personal space to be auspicious, it must have proper shelter so that you are protected from the elements - the wind, the rain and the sun.

The triangle roof line

Houses with flat roofs are deemed to have inadequate shelter. It is therefore advisable to build a proper roof. The usual <u>triangular shape</u> is excellent because it allows excess water to flow down and not collect on the rooftop. This triangle however can cause problems to neighbours if the peak of the triangle directly points at someone's door. Try not to let this happen since your neighbour could use a Pa Kua mirror to counter your roof, in the process sending harmful energy your way.

A word about Blue roof tiles
One of the four danger indications in the I Ching has to do with the concept of *water on top of mountain.*
According to feng shui masters, water on top of mountain breaks its banks and spills over causing loss, hunger and death.
Water on the roof is therefore considered as extremely bad feng shui. Blue rooftiles symbolize water and I have seen residents of such houses suffer horrendous losses and heartbreak. I therefore strongly advise against the use of blue or black tiles. The best tiles to use for the roof should be maroon coloured or red.

A word about Pyramid roofs
In recent years this shaped roof has become popular. The pyramid shape is a mysteriously powerful shape that has extremely wonderful yin energies.

Because of this, it is extremely auspicious when used for museums and other places that benefit from *yin* energy.
They are not suitable for *yang* dwellings, and indeed, could well cause you losses, illness and death. They are unsuitable for office blocks and shopping complexes.

CHAPTER
SIX

FENG SHUI
FOR
DIFFERENT
ROOMS IN
THE HOME

TIPS FOR
HOUSE
ELEVATIONS

Don't have too many corners | TIP 167

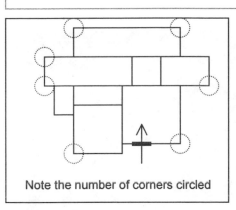

Note the number of corners circled

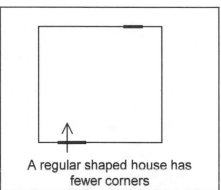

A regular shaped house has fewer corners

Houses and buildings that have too many corners resemble a *porcupine*, sending out sharp arrows outwards. This is because there will be so many sharp edges creating and shooting out *killing energy*. Neighbours are certain to be negatively affected by these arrows, and are bound to retaliate. In the end both you and your neighbours suffer from bad energy which bring extreme bad luck.

When designing the elevations of your home therefore do try to reduce the number of corners. In the sketch plans above, the plan on the right is better from a feng shui perspective, than the plan on the left precisely because it has less number of corners, and therefore its shape is more regular.

The feng shui of pillars
The elevations of Pillars on the ground floor may look visually pleasing but from a feng shui perspective, they are most inauspicious. These pillars with no walls cause all the *chi* to flow right through. Nothing can be retained. The *chi* cannot accumulate.

Businesses located in such buildings seldom survive more than three years . The foundation is missing. Close up with walls and fill the ground floor with shops or office rooms.

CHAPTER
SIX

FENG SHUI
FOR
DIFFERENT
ROOMS IN
THE HOME

TIPS FOR
ENHANCING
FENG SHUI
LUCK

My feng shui energizers | TIP 168

Feng shui can be great fun and I want to share all the things that I have used in the past twenty years to activate the corners of my house with such success. In my home, you will find all the feng shui energizers that I recommend in my books, and in these last few pages of this book I want to tell you about some of the more potent energizers that I have used.

AA:
A crystal chandelier ten feet inside the foyer to attract in the good chi.

BB:
A painting of a girl playing the flute to welcome in the good *sheng chi*

CC:
A painting of a waterfall with the

seeming to come from the NORTH direction. The waterfall is also pouring its water into my real fishpond below.

DD:
The windchime here is to activate the luck of this corner of the house.

EE:
This is one of the Chinese Gods of wealth – Kuan Kung. He is also a protective deity. His presence in the home symbolizes good wealth luck.

FF:
Healthy green plants to bring in the garden. Plants are always lucky if they grow lush and healthy. All the symbols used in this foyer area create a healthy basket of elements.

CHAPTER
SIX

FENG SHUI
FOR
DIFFERENT
ROOMS IN
THE HOME

TIPS FOR
HOUSE
ELEVATIONS

Globes and Gem trees for success | TIP 169

For success in business, a very powerful earth energizer is the globe.
If you belong to the WEST group direction (see page 2 to check) then placing a globe in the West, **Southwest or Northeast** corner of your house will bring you enormous business luck especially if you twirl the globe three times daily.

GEM TREES

This tip is also for a West group person. Place a gem tree in the West, Southwest or Northeast to activate all the business luck you need.

Manufacturers in South Africa and Brazil are presently making these gem trees. Semi precious stones must be used as leaves and the branches must be made of silver with gold plating. It is therefore symbolic of a tree studded with precious stones that represent wealth.
The stones represent the earth element, and it is from the earth that gold is found.

CHAPTER
SIX

FENG SHUI
FOR
DIFFERENT
ROOMS IN
THE HOME

TIPS FOR
ENHANCING
FENG SHUI
LUCK

And finally, my personal favourites | TIP 170

I keep an entire family of mandarin ducks (made of wood) in a sideboard in the center of my home, in the family room upstairs. This ensures that my immediate and extended family stays close. A pair of mandarin ducks is an excellent symbol for newlyweds as they symbolize love and fidelity in a marriage.

I am also a great believer in the feng shui symbolism of the tortoise simply because I have seen it work everytime. So in addition to my pet terrapins and tortoise I also have a collection of fake tortoises which I place in the North corner of every room in my home. Here are three of them.

In the last two years I have been receiving increasing amounts of feng shui mail from my readers from all over the world. Many of you reach me via email and fax, and many of you have mostly the same questions. I am therefore reproducing here some of the more frequently asked questions.

Question: We live in the Southern Hemisphere. Do we need to change the directions around to take account of the different wind systems in the South ?

Answer: Not at all. This question has cropped up frequently and on many occasions I have had to explain that the North that is referred to in Chinese feng shui is the same magnetic North whether you live in the north or the south hemisphere. The confusion for this arose many years ago when a feng shui writer from the West speculated that the reason the South was symbolic of fire and warmth was because the equator lay south of China. Thus, he wrote that the element of the south was *fire*. This led feng shui enthusiasts to conclude that if that was the explanation then people living in the south would have to change south into north since the equator lies north of all countries in the southern hemisphere.

However the real reason the south is equated with fire in feng shui is NOT because of the location of the equator, but rather to the arrangement of the 8 trigrams around the Pa Kua. The trigram *li* is placed in the south under the later heaven arrangement of the trigrams and since this is the arrangement that is used for the analysis of feng shui for yang dwellings (houses of the living) we equate the element of this trigram to the direction south. The element of the trigram li is fire ! Thus it is unnecessary to make any changes to the direction analysis if you live in the Southern Hemisphere.

Question: With so many different schools of feng shui I am confused, Which school or method should we follow and can we mix the methods ?

Answer: It is understandable that confusion will result from the proliferation of feng shui books and "experts" in recent years. Basically however there are only two schools of feng shui – the form or landscape school and the compass or formula school. It is acceptable to use several methods together since authentic feng shui is based on the same fundamentals for interpretation and for formulating corrections or antidotes to bad feng shui. When in doubt examine the credentials of the source person who is giving you the feng shui advice. Genuine feng shui masters are usually very understated and reticent about their knowledge. But they have a portfolio of satisfied clients and disciples. And they themselves are very successful.

Question: I have been reading about East and West group persons, and the directions that are auspicious for the two groups differ. What if my husband and I belong to different groups ?

Answer: This is a very common difficulty faced by couples who belong to different groups and thus have different KUA numbers. Everything that is excellent and auspicious for one will be extremely unlucky for the other. In feng shui, whenever you have to choose between the husband and the wife's direction you always go with the husband's direction. I always advice my friends and readers to arrange their feng shui according to the KUA number of the breadwinner and if this is the wife so be it ! In my house I have two doors, one for my husband and one for me, and wherever possible I have designed my feng shui to benefit both my husband and I, even though we belong to different groups. Thus I have my own bathroom, my own room, my own rice pot and so on ... and does my husband. It has worked very well for us.

Question: Which is more important – the outside feng shui or the inside feng shui; the garden or the interior decoration of my house ?

Answer: Both are as important but because outside feng shui is harder to correct it is worthwhile to get the outside properly investigated for feng shui flaws before deciding on a house of apartment. Inside the house, almost everything that is wrong from a feng shui perspective can be corrected. But feng shui problems on the outside are not as easy to correct. And because negative feng shui is always more powerful than positive feng shui, when there is something wrong on the outside, all the good feng shui you do on the inside will simply be overwhelmed. So take care of the feng shui of your immediate outside environment first.

Question: How do I use the Chinese feng shui compass ?

Answer: It is not necessary to use the Chinese feng shui compass at all. The Luo Pan is impossible to read or understand unless you read Chinese and have a feng shui master who is prepared to reveal to you all the meanings of all the codes. Also, the Chinese feng shui compass is not a standard compass. Every genuine master has his own compass. For amateur feng shui practice however, a good Western compass is better. Arm yourself with a comprehensive book on compass school feng shui, learn up the methods and the formulas, then use a western compass to give you accurate readings. It is definitely worthwhile to invest in a good accurate compass.

Question: There are so many different books on feng shui. Is it necessary to read all the books to be able to practice on my own ?

Answer: If you read a really complete introductory book on feng shui there is no need to buy other books if all you want to do is arrange your own feng shui. You should start with a good introductory book on feng shui and get the more advanced books only after you have mastered the basic fundamentals of feng shui. Take it slowly and go step by step.

Question: What if I lack the confidence to do my own feng shui ? Should I consult a professional feng shui man ?

Answer: This is a very personal decision. I discovered how easy feng shui was many years ago, and I have been doing my own feng shui for well over 20 years even though my good friend Yap Cheng Hai was always there for me if and when I needed him. These days feng shui consultants have become very expensive and it might be better to learn to do it yourself. I can tell you for certain that 90% of today's feng shui consultants learnt from the books available. You can too!

Question: Does feng shui always work ? What if I activate my career corner but nothing happens. How long do I have to wait for it to work ?

Answer: In my experience with feng shui over the past thirty years, it has always worked for me. The degree of good luck varies from time to time but whenever I consciously set out to improve my luck through feng shui, it has never failed me. I have also not had a failure in all the years of helping my friends get over specific problems at any moment in time.

If you energize any particular corner, or start using the KUA formula in the many different ways I have suggested in this book. You should be able to see a difference within four to six weeks. Feng shui usually works quite fast, although the speed with which you see results can vary depending on the astrological chart. There is such a thing as *heaven luck* which overrides feng shui luck.

Question: How do I know if I am suffering from bad feng shui ?

Answer: You know that something is wrong when you get sick more frequently, when several negative things happen to you suddenly, when you lose your job for no reason. When you have a series of accidents. It doesn't hurt to check out your feng shui then.

Question: If I have bad feng shui should I make changes even though I am renting the house that I am staying in ?

Answer: If you can move out and find another place, that is always the best solution. But if you have signed a long lease, or have about a year to go before you can move out then I advise you to do something about your feng shui if you know exactly what is wrong. Sometimes the feng shui cure involves very little effort. Just hanging a mirror or a Pa Kua is often sufficient to deflect a poison arrow.

Question: What if my front door faces a hill, and I cannot change the location or direction of my door ?

Answer: There are certainly many feng shui problems that simply cannot be corrected. It is not possible to move a mountain that is located right in front of the house. In such a case, put a sign on your main door saying BACK DOOR to " fool" the energies. Then build windows on the wall that is at the real back of the house. This should tap the mountain as your protector. In feng shui you really have to think through your problems.

Question: I have heard that feng shui luck can also change over time. If this is so how do I know when my luck has changed ?

Answer: The time dimension in feng shui luck is defined as the period luck. In feng shui, time periods define good and bad times, which lasts for 20 years at a stretch. The present 20 year period started in 1983 and will end in the year 2003. Houses have their own natal charts and these can be calculated according to a special formula called *flying star feng shui*. When you have studied enough feng shui and want to become more advanced I recommend you start to learn flying star feng shui since this is the divinitive branch of feng shui. It is extremely accurate but also difficult to learn correctly. I have a whole book written just on the flying star formula.

Question: How do I cope with contradictory feng shui advice

Answer: It is simply impossible to get one's feng shui 100% correct. Thus while I may advise you to follow the directions that are auspicious for you, it may be that by following my advice you will inadvertently come face to face with a poison arrow, which I also ask you to avoid. My advice would seem to be contradictory. In such cases you should go with the particular feng shui option that will cause you less harm. Thus you should avoid the poison arrow even if it means a less auspicious direction.

Question: Is there a method of feng shui for helping the children to study and get better grades at school ?

Answer: I have discovered that if you energize the Northeast corner of your child's bedroom, he/she will definitely study better, work harder and reap better results at school or college. Another method is for the child to sit facing his/her education direction. This formula is in the first chapter of this book. If you missed it please do go back to look for it and then try it with your children. You will be pleasantly surprised at how fast feng shui works.

Question: I read somewhere that you say if there is a toilet in the SW corner it will ruin all the romance in my life. I do have a toilet in the SW of my flat. Is that why I am still unmarried and cannot seem to find the right girl ? I am 37.

Answer: You should try to stop using this toilet of yours. If this is the only toilet in your apartment and you absolutely must use it, then I suggest you place a large piece of log in the toilet to counter the effect of the negative energies that is creating bad luck in your love life. This solution applies the five element theory to overcome what is really a difficult problem. In the old days in China, homes had no toilets. Wealthy families who could afford had their toilets and baths brought to them by servants. The peasant class built their toilets a little way away from the main house.

Question: Are you saying that all toilets are bad ?

Answer: Indeed yes. There is no place in the home where the toilets do not do some kind of harm. This is why I always recommend that toilets be made as small and as unobtrusive as possible. The WC itself should ideally be kept out of sight. Use a curtain or a low wall to achieve this.

If the toilet is in the East and Southeast it has a negative effect on the health and wealth of residents. To counter the bad result of this toilet, hang a curved knife in the toilet. This will symbolically destroy the negative energies of the toilet.

Question: What if the toilet is in the South of my house ?

Answer: If your toilet is in the south your reputation will suffer. To counter the bad energy of this toilet, you should place a large urn kept full with water – right to the brim.

Question: Can I use feng shui to win the lottery?

Answer: I have never tested this out so I really cannot say. But next time you sit down for a game of bridge or mahjong, try the tip I have given on sitting directions that are based on your lucky KUA number. I once used this KUA formula at a casino in Brisbane where I was attending a Convention to try to make back the two hundred dollars I had lost the previous night. Happily the KUA formula did indeed work. Having said this I have to say that I am not at all sure that this will happen everytime.

Question: Can feng shui really help me get a better social life ?

Answer: There are specific feng shui guidelines for improving one's family life and social relationships. The best method is to sue the KUA formula but this can be supplemented by using symbolic emblems of love, romance and relationships. If you energize the love and relationship corners of your room, your social life will improve. If you are looking for marriage, that too is possible. Feng shui can bring you the opportunities but it does not guarantee that you will necessarily get a compatible wife or husband. That depends on your other types of luck.

Question: Do I have to redo at my feng shui every year

Answer: It is not necessary to redo your feng shui every year but it is advisable to do so. I look at my feng shui almost every day. Thus I shape my trees regularly; cut the grass every fourteen days and move my furniture around each New year. I even undertake renovations each Spring to keep the energies in my house alive and well. I observe all the taboos about dates and being careful about certain directions. You should look at feng shui as a fun thing to do. It should not be a chore.

Question: So how do I go about calculating the taboo dates and taboo directions to avoid each year ...

Answer: It is possible to learn this more advanced part of compass feng shui. When you feel sufficiently confident you might want to check out my three feng shui formula books. Good luck to you.
The formula books are :
- Chinese Numerology in Feng shui (contains the flying star formula)
- Applied pa Kua Lo Shu feng shui (contains the KUA formula)
- Water feng shui for wealth (contains the water dragon formula)